The SOSTAC® Guide To Your Perfect Digital Marketing Plan

by PR Smith

D1338903

About The Author

Paul enjoys exploring new approaches to marketing

Paul runs workshops, advises and mentors as well as writes books about digital marketing. Someone once told hm that there were 17,000 Paul Smiths in the UK alone, so with his initial being 'R', he adopted PR Smith as his pen name.

Workshops

Paul's workshops, webinars and conference talks have been described as 'Inspirational, innovative, insightful' and are always delivered in a carefully structured method so that key points are easily remembered and, more importantly, actioned. Although intense sessions, delegates have fun too.

Adviser/Mentor

Whether developing digital marketing strategies and integrated plans, mobilizing social media teams or delivering websites, Paul has helped to boost the results of, literally, hundreds of organisations from blue chips to innovative SMEs, whether mentoring, consulting or on an advisory board.

Books

His six books are published in seven languages. America's Jim Sterne refers to Emarketing Excellence 4th Ed. as '*a must read*'. The CIM refer to Marketing Communications 5th Ed as a '*Marketing Major*'. While SOSTAC® Planning is voted in the top 3 marketing models worldwide.

Paul's Personal Passion – The Great Sportsmanship Programme

A social media-driven campaign to change the world by mobilising a new generation of youths into sportsmanship values. Built around inspirational and true two minute stories (watch the video) on www.GreatSportsmanship.org. It's a very different edutainment programme. Join us as an ambassador or just enjoy the stories. Pass them on.

Academia

PR Smith is a visiting lecturer in the Cass Business School (London), the Dublin Institute of Technology and he speaks in Europe, the Middle East and the USA. He is a Fellow of the Chartered Institute of Marketing and a member of the Chartered Institute of Public Relations, with a BSc Management from Dublin University, a PG Dip Finance from Southbank University and an MBA from Cass Business School.

Interests

Paul is 30 years happily married to Beverley whom he says, "is the most patient wife in the world". They have three, now adult, children. Paul enjoys music and travel, plays football, touch rugby, golf and sport in general. He is author of Great Moments Of Sportsmanship and founder of The Great Sportsmanship Programme (NFP) which is designed to nurture a new generation of global citizens into sportsmanship values.

- PRSmith.org
- PR Smith Marketing
- @PR_Smith
- PR Smith Marketing
- PRSmith1000

SOSTAC® The Guide To Your Perfect Digital Marketing Plan

Contents

Acknowledgments 7
Preface 11
Introduction to SOSTAC® 15
Chapter 1 18
Situation Analysis 18
Situation Analysis Is Critical To Future Success 19
1.1 Customer Analysis...22
   1.1.1 Who...25
   1.1.2 Why? 51
   1.1.3 How? 66
1.3 Partners and Intermediaries 99
1.4 Competencies Analysis.......................................101
1.5 Performance/Results Analysis 103
1.6 Market Trends – opportunities and threats 108
Chapter 2 116
Objectives 116
2.1 Mission 117
2.2 Vision...117
2.3 KPIs 118
2.4 The Race Approach to Objectives 124
2.5 The 5Ss Approach To Objectives 125
2.6 Inspirational Objectives 125
Chapter 3 130
Strategy..130
3.1 Strategy – The Difference: Success and Failure ...132
3.2 Positioning and Your Online Value Proposition ..138
3.3 Components of Digital Marketing Strategy 140
3.4 Sample Strategy Excerpts 149
3.5 Your Strategy Template.......................................152
3.6 Your Strategy Checklist.......................................156

Chapter 4 159
Tactics 159
  4.1 Tactical Tools and The Marketing Mix 160
  4.2 Ten Tactical Tools - Offline and Online................162
  4.3 Ten Tactical Tools Primary Objectives 163
  4.4 Which Tactical Tools Should You Use? 167
  4.5 Which Tactical Tools -The Tactical Matrix 175
  4.6 Which Tactical Tools and When 179
  4.7 Tactical Targeting - More Bang For Your Buck ..183
  4.8 The Magic Marketing Formula.............................191
Chapter 5 196
Actions 196
  5.1 Mini Action Plans..200
  5.2 Systems e.g. Content Marketing.........................202
  5.3 Systems e.g. Marketing Automation System.......207
  5.4 Processes e.g. RFM Database Analysis..............210
  5.5 Guidelines - social media guidelines 212
  5.6 Checklists – social media checklist 217
  5.7 Constant small improvements..............................218
  5.7 Internal marketing...221
Chapter 6 225
Control...225
  6.1 Building 'control' into your plan.......................226
  6.2 Measuring the KPIs 227
  6.2 Is your website under control?............................235
  6.3 Is your marketing content under control?...........242
  6.4 Is your share of voice under control?..................243
  6.5 Developing a constant beta culture.....................244
  6.6 Constant learnings and insights 245
  6.7 90 Day Planning 249
Summary 251
  Appendices 255
  References...285
  A Final Word 292

Acknowledgments

Many thanks to Hugo Rubio for really pushing me to write the original SOSTAC® Guide. I have been asked many times to do it by other people but Hugo was the most persuasive. He flew over from Bilbao, sat down andtalked me through why I should write this. Hugo has also helped me to improve the content in many different ways. Un saludo Hugo.

My thanks to Dave Chaffey (Smart Insights) with whom I have co-authored Emarketing Excellence. Dave & I discuss SOSTAC® intensely regularly and Dave's feedback has been invaluable. Thanks to Davy McDonald (book cover) and Brian O'Neill (web site) with whom I work closely on many digital marketing projects around the world. Thanks to Mohamed Sameh, Digital Marketing Manager, ITV Agency with whom I've been discussing the Tactical Matrix. Thanks also to Mike Hollingsworth for the internal graphics. In summary, thanks to:

Dr. Anthony Buckley, Dublin Institute of Technology
Beverly Barker, Course Leader IDM
Mike Berry, Coure Leader IDM
Ged Carroll, Digital Director VP Europe, RacePoint Global
Dr. Dave Chaffey, CEO Smart Insights
Osama Fawsi, Business Development Manager, ITV Agency
Andy Fernandez, Bookshop and Library Manager CIM
David Green, Head Of Global Digital Digital Marketing, KPMG

Colm Hannon, Hannon Digital & founder, The Rugby Business Network
Mike Hollingsworth, Graphic & Web Design
John Horseley, Chairman, Digital Doughnut
Dr. Etain Kidney, Dublin Institute of Technology
Jez Lysaght, Brand & Communications Director, New Projects, Transdev London
Bernard Marr, CEO, The Advanced Performance Institute
Ian Maynard, MD, Ian Maynard Marketing
John McGrann, CEO, Drive Social Media
Paul O'Sullivan, Dean, Dublin Institute Technology
Charles Randall, Head of Solutions Marketing, SAS
Hugo Rubio, IBM, Spain
Ahmed Sabry, CEO Digital Marketing Arts Academy
Mohamed Sameh, Digital Marketing Manager, ITV Agency
Ben Salmon, Marketing Data Technologist
Richard Sedley, Partner & Client Services Director, Seren
Adam Sharp, MD, Clever-Touch.com
Adam Smith, Marketing Manager, ZenithOptimedia
Jay Thorogood-Cooper, CEO Bloom Worldwide
Tom Trainor, CEO, the Marketing Institute of Irel&
Jon Twomey, MD, Student Support Group
Ze Zook, co author, Marketing Communications

Thanks also to the ever patient and lovely Beverley who puts up with me locking myself in my study for months so that I could produce this, at last, the SOSTAC® Guide To Writing the Perfect Digital Marketing Plan.

Feedback

All feedback is most welcome via the form on my website www.PRSmith.org/feedback . Please allow me to apologise, in advance, for any inconsistencies in the layout and style as this is a new form of self publishing and your patience is very much appreciated. But please do send feedback.

Thank you for sending interesting content

Much other content, links, videos, articles and tweets that people send me are shared on my various social media platforms (see below). Thank you to those of you who alert me to interesting articles, reports, videos, blog posts, Facbook updates and tweets. I particularly seek examples of creative marketing, ideally driven by analytics or market research, that delivers great results. I am constantly seeking examples to update this book and my other books.

You can get updates, discuss posts and tweets or contact me about advising, coaching or speaking at your next event via any of the links below.

PRSmith.org

PRSmith Marketing

@PR_Smith

PR Smith Marketing

PRSmith1000

And if you like honour, nobility, integrity, respect, sport and a lot more, please join me in our social-media-driven  campaign to change theworld, bit by bit, by inspiring youths and whole communities into sportsmanship values via inspirational true two-minute stories about sportsmanship.

The Great Sportsmanship Programme comprises several social media platforms, a book and an educational programme that boosts literacy, self esteem & social behaviour.

 GreatSportsmanship.org

 GreatSportsmanship

 GtSportsmanship

 Great Sportsmanship Programme

 Great Sportsmanship Programme

Preface

Although this is a quick guide to writing the perfect digital marketing plan it has taken many years to write it as a short guide. I have used SOSTAC® in all of my marketing plans and clients love it. I also use it in all of my text books in various editions over the years including:

- eMarketing eXcellence – planning and optimising your digital marketing

- Marketing Communications – integrating offline and online with social media

Why use SOSTAC®?

SOSTAC® is a
- simple
- clear
- logical
- memorable
- structure

It can be used as a template that ensures consistency when presenting plans from different teams, departments or regional offices throughout an organisation whether local, natonal or global.

People like SOSTAC® as it clarifies and simplifies the planning process for everyone. It can be learned in four minutes, or explored in full detail in four hours.

SOSTAC® is flexible

You can adapt SOSTAC® anyway you want. You can move a lot of the Situation Analysis into the Appendices if you prefer. Use your own approach to writing your preferred Objectives. The most flexible section is 'Strategy' where I list the key components to consider. You may prefer to use just a handful of these components to develop a great strategy (as long as you have at least considered all the key components I list). Some people juggle subsections of Tactics with the Action section. That's fine. Use SOSTAC® to build your own solid logical plan. In fact, some of you may notice some variation of the acronym I use to remember the key components of strategy in various editions of various books of mine. This book contains the latest and, I believe it to be the best.

How did SOSTAC® evolve?

Although SOSTAC® is simple, it actually took me almost 10 years to develop. When I took my MBA back in the 1980s I was frustrated reading books with long meandering marketing plans that were unnecessarily over-complicated and impossible to remember. So I kept in touch with my classmates and asked them to send me just the contents page (list of contents) from their marketing plans. I analysed all of them over a two year period and developed my own new structure – which went through several iterations for several years until I came up with SOSTAC®.

 It was like someone had turned the light on! I knew it was a winner and registered it as a trademark. If you are referring to SOSTAC® please include the full reference as follows: 'PR Smith's SOSTAC®'.

Please embed this url www.PRSmith.org/sostac so that the reference appears as follows: PR Smith's SOSTAC® .

Who can use this book and how can you use it?
Experienced digital marketers will be familiar with a lot of the content in this book, so they may find just dipping in and out to check how SOSTAC® approaches a particular part of the plan e.g. Chapter 3 on Strategy may provide one or two extra dimensions to consider when building a digital strategy. There is also some cassic board room strategy discussed in the appendices. Less experienced digital marketers can scan cover to cover in one hour and return to each section and follow the links in more detail to embed and deepen their knowledge.

Where does SOSTAC® Digital Marketing Plan fit with the Main Marketing Plan?
As more and more customers migrate online, so too, more and more of the marketing budget is allocated to digital marketing which means that many managers are now asked to present their digital marketing plans separately. Ultimately, online and offline will integrate and marketers will instinctively leverage online with offline and vice versa.

Eventually we won't have digital marketing plans (it'll just be integrated marketing plans) but right now, managers are being asked to present their digital marketing plans – hence this short guide which really gives you a great structure and insights for your digital marketing plan. It also works for any other type of plan.

I really do hope you enjoy this guide and that it helps you to write your own perfect digital marketing plan. As always, I welcome any feedback – please post it on www.prsmith.org/feedback . And perhaps continue the conversation on twitter or any of the platforms already mentioned.

I look forward to hearing from you.
Best wishes
PR Smith

Introduction to SOSTAC®

So here it is SOSTAC® + 3Ms in one minute.

Situation Analysis – where are we now?
Objectives – where do we want to get to?
Strategy – how do we get there?
Tactics – the details of strategy
Action – the details of tactics (systems, processes, guidelines and checklists)
Control – measurement and metrics to see if 'we are getting there' or not

+ 3Ms (the three key resources):
- Men and Women (human resources);
- Money (budgets);
- Minutes (time scales)

And now, if you want, you can see this on video, in a bit more detail, in four minutes via the web site on the next page, or watch it later and continue with the book.

Visit www.PRSmith.org/SOSTAC
& watch the 4 minute video.

SOSTAC® is a registered trade mark of www.PRSmith.org

PR Smith's SOSTAC® Plan

Chapter 1

Situation Analysis

SOSTAC® is a registered trade mark of www.PRSmith.org

Situation Analysis Is Critical To Future Success

Arguably, the greatest marketing book ever, was written over 2,000 years ago. The Chinese military strategist Sun Tzu wrote *The Art of War* (translated version Wing, 1989). Most senior marketers have a copy of it on their shelves. It has become a classic read, particularly for some enlightened marketing managers. Interestingly confrontation, or war, is seen as a last resort and the best military strategies win the war without any bloodshed. They win wars through intelligence.

Sun Tzu effectively confirms why the Situation Analysis needs to be comprehensive.
Here's an excerpt:

Those who triumph,
Compute at their headquarters
a great number of factors
prior to a challenge.

Those who are defeated,
compute at their headquarters
a small number of factors
prior to a challenge.

Much computation brings triumph.
Little computation brings defeat.
How much more so with no computation at all.

By observing only this,
I can see triumph or defeat.

'Much Computation' or much analysis is required. The better the analysis, the easier the decisions will be later. Decisions about strategy and tactics become a lot easier when you know your customers, your competitors, your competencies and resources as well as market trends. That's why half your plan should be devoted to the Situation Analysis. It doesn't have to be at the front of the plan (you can dump a lot of it in the appendices) but the detailed analysis must be carried out if you are to succeed.

Hence almost half of this guide is devoted to Situation Analysis. The first year you do this analysis – it will be particularly challenging, but as you find better (and often free) resources for highly relevant information, this analysis gets easier, the intelligent information gets stronger and consequently, you make better informed decisions. This ultimately boosts your results.

More good news – there is a plethora of new listening tools available to marketers. Although traditional market research is still useful, there are faster ways of monitoring online discussions and analysing customers, competitors and spotting trends. We will explore these.

"All markets are conversations"
Declared the influential Cluetrain Manifesto (Levine et al, 2000). The subsequent rampant growth of social media since that time confirms the classic Cluetrain vision.

The Old Marketing Ship Is Sinking

All marketers need to monitor, analyse and engage in these conversations since the old 'shouting' model (advertising and PR) is no longer as effective as it once was.

Today's marketing models involves careful listening to customers (and prospects) online (as well as offline) and giving fast responses to changing moods, needs, issues and trends that are occurring online continually. Marketers don't have a choice. This is not a luxury set of tools. These new listening tools are 'must haves'. See <u>Social Listening Skills</u> for more information on each of the tools discussed on the next few pages.

The Old Marketing Ship Is Sinking
Photo courtesy of <u>DavyMac.com</u>

What Should The Situation Analysis Contain?

Your Situation Analysis should be so thorough that it makes your decisions almost risk-free.

Your Situation Analysis should contain a thorough analysis of:
- Customers

- Competitors
- Partners (and intermediaries)
- Competencies
- Performance/Results
- Market trends

1.1 *Customer Analysis*

So let's start with the centre of the universe, well, the centre of the marketing universe, 'customers'. Your Customer Analysis needs to be so thorough that it ensures you **know your customers better than they know themselves**.

If you could only ask three questions about your customers– what would you ask?
If you could only ask three questions about your customers, what would those three questions be? Marketers have limited resources, the 3Ms: Men (and Women), Money and Minutes. A Limited number of people (men and women) who can help you find this information. Limited budget (money) to hire people, commission market research or buy reports. Limited time (minutes) to search, find, collect and digest the information. So, you have to choose your questions carefully.

How You Can Make Better Decisions
Before making any major decision, ask yourself, 'Do I have all the information I need to make a great decision?'
In other words what questions do I need to ask before I make a decision?

What would you ask?
Try these three big customer questions:
- Who?
- Why?
- How?

You'll find that most questions about customers will fall into these three categories. So if you can master these questions, I mean, get detailed answers, then you'll find choosing which channels and which marketing tactics becomes a lot easier, and your marketing results will, ultimately, improve.

'Who' usually gets the weakest answer
Who exactly is my ideal customer or visitor (or prospect or decision maker)? This is often unclear or even undefined when making marketing decisions. What kind of traffic do you want to attract? What is the profile of existing customers? How can you find your ideal customer if you don't know who they are? It's like 'looking for a needle in a haystack' except you don't know what the needle looks like! So you've got little or no chance of finding it unless you spend an unnecessary large amount of resources. This is 'hit-and-miss' marketing, or worse still, 'hit and hope' marketing. We'll look at defining segments and using personas to precisely answer this question more later in this section.

'Why' is the most difficult of all three questions
Because customers often don't know and don't tell you 'why' they buy or don't buy, or why they register or don't register, or why they follow, like, share, visit, stay, bounce (leave quickly) or return to your site. Many customers themselves, don't even know why

they buy. There are often unconscious reasons driving their behaviour. Ask people why they drink Coke or why they 'Like' Coke's Facbook page and they almost always give rational reasons when, in fact, it's for mostly emotional reasons (I know you probably disagree – now do you get my point?).

'How' do customers buy?
Includes 'what is their digital journey?' or if you prefer, what is their 'multichannel path to purchase?' What route do they take (via search engine, PPC Ads, website, referral site or any other mix)? How many visits? When do they search for information, when do they decide and when do they buy? All of these questions generate answers to another question: 'when is the best time to post content?' How do customers change channels, say between reading offline media and interacting with online media and then visiting a physical location? Equally, 'What are my competitor's prices?' might be categorised under 'How' much do my competitors' customers pay?

Become customer obsessed and master the 'Who, Why and How' questions
You can categorise whatever way you prefer, but either way, Who, Why and How may help you to categorise and remember at least these three big questions. It may help you to remember many of the other questions you want to ask about your customers.
Master these questions and you are taking your first step towards being a world class marketer. Put it another way, without in-depth answers to these three big key customer questions you are playing a

dangerous guessing game, while your competitors may be discovering and using valuable customer insights to gain competitive advantage via understanding, then serving and nurturing stronger relations) simply because they know your customers better than you do. Make your organisation customer obsessed.

Now let's look at each of these in more detail and start with the question that many marketers cannot answer: 'Who is your ideal customer?'

Most Marketers Don't Fully Know Who Their Customers Are

Only 45% of marketers are capturing and consolidating customer behavioural data from multiple channels in a single database (Forrester, 2013).

1.1.1 Who

Defining who your ideal customer is makes it a lot easier to find new customers and to decide which types of customers are worth spending resources on. In summary, Customer Profiling helps prospecting, winning and retaining profitable customers.

Who is the ideal customer who will be pleased to hear from you (as opposed to feeling disturbed by your intrusion and therefore not having the time nor interest in your special message)? What is the 'ideal customer' profile? Can you clearly define them? Who are your Facbook visitors, your LinkedIn visitors, your Youtube viewers, your Instagram sharers and your website visitors?

Are You Searching For (an invisible) Needle in A Hay Stack?

If you can't define clearly who exactly is your ideal customer, how can you ever find them? It's like looking for a needle in a haystack, except you don't know what you are looking for since you don't have a clear customer description or profile. You may as well be looking in the dark, but not knowing what you are looking for!

Not knowing your customers is like marketing with a blindfold on!

Don't let yourself become another fool in the dark, continually searching for customers without being really sure who you are looking for, what they look like or what their profile is.

Don't be another fool in the dark marketing with a blindfold

Knowing who your ideal customer is - makes finding new customers easier

Once you have clearly defined the profile(s) of your ideal customer(s), it now becomes easier to find similar 'ideal customers'. Without a clear definition you are looking for a needle in a haystack (and you don't know what the needle looks like!) A well-defined customer profile, stops all the aimless searching. Combining some of the new targeting tools and new databases, with clearly defined 'ideal customer' profiles saves you time and money and boosts results when we look at targeting in the Tactics section.

In addition to the old B2C demographics (job, age, gender, location, income etc.) we can now add psychographics (interests, attitudes and personality attributes) as well as technographics (their technical and online click behaviour can reveal their needs and more). Where and when do they go online? On which device(s)? What kind of content do they engage with? What do they share? Which ones share?

Business to business (B2B) segmentation variables typically include: industry sector, job type, size of company, location, centralised or decentralised, benefits sought and even attitude to risk. Today we can add new variables like interests (pages viewed), topics discussed and more. Depending on the number of market sectors you operate in, you may have more than one type of 'ideal customer'. More on this later.

So let's start with some 'Who' questions:

- Who is your ideal customer?
- Who are your visitors and what stage of the buying process are they at?
- Who are your followers?
- Who are your influential customers, visitors and followers?
- Who else is talking about your type of product (and what are they saying)?
- Who is attending a particular conference or event (and what are they saying)?
- Ask your data and you shall receive

Who is your ideal customer?

Having converted a percentage of your visitors to customers and entered them onto your database, the next question is: who are your best customers? Which ones are more likely to respond to your offers? Which ones should you target with special offers? For many decades now, database marketers have used RFM (Recency, Frequency, Monetary) to help to identify those active customers that are more likely to continue buying throughout their customer lifetime. See Tactics for more on RFM.

> "I've spent most of my life not knowing who the customer is. Isn't that a shame?" Lyor Cohen director at Island Def Jam & Warner Music Group.
>
> (Sisario, 2014)

Personas

Personas bring target segments to life by describing, in more detail, the different types of customers that exist within a segment. As well as the usual demographics, personas include favourite media, type of car, partner's job type and interests, webographics (web experience, usage, location, platform) plus a statement related to the product such as: 'I've got loads of ideas and enthusiasm, I just don't know where to start.' Three or four personas are usually enough. The primary persona should be an important customer for the business plus 'needy' from a design point of view (e.g. 'technically challenged' or a 'beginner user'). Personas have been used in advertising for decades. Today's digital marketers use personas to focus on delivering the right content, website and overall online experience.

Personas
A thumbnail summary of the characteristics, needs, motivations and environment of typical website users.

Here is a heuristic persona template from Steve Jackson, Cult of Analytics (2011). It basically covers Tasks prior to purchase; Considerations and questions; Pain points; Search terms; Key paths/content.

Goals	Insert Goal - Determine your persona's key motivation or reason for visiting your website. Note that it's the persona's goal not necessarily your business goal. This data about key motivations comes from the research stage.
Scenario	**Describe the persona's typical scenario and reasoning for visiting your site.** • What would be the typical way that the persona would know about your product or service? • How would they find out about the product or service? • What specific methods are involved in reaching you? • How would the person do his/her research?
Tasks prior to purchase	Tasks prior to taking action – • Determine all the tasks the persona will need to accomplish before being in a position to take the action you want them to take. • What does he/she need to find out? • What is his/her first major concern about the product or service? • What are the next 4 factors that need to be understood in order to

	have a better idea of all the risks involved?
Considerations and questions	**Considerations** • From the scenario and the task list determine what questions your persona may have about your product or service. • It should be relatively easy at this point to come up with around 10 key questions that the persona would want answered before deciding to purchase.
Pain points	**Pain points** • Will be different for each persona and very personal. • What makes the persona cry out in frustration? • If he/she is potentially defecting from one product or service to yours, what pains him about the current situation? • If not, what are the needs that

	really pain him/her the most?
Search terms	**Based on the pain points and considerations** • Trigger terms are words people look for or use to try and solve their problems. • Used in search engines, on blog posts, in emails. • Determine 5 terms that will be used to search on search engines that relate to the pain points and problem the persona has. It's good to do prior research around these keywords on Google Keyword tools.
Key paths/ content	• **Determine the paths** that the user has to take to answer all of the questions/considerations and solve all the pain points the user has.

Here is a completed persona for Tapio

He is a 36 year old Finnish entrepreneur working for himself. Often working on the road, in the office or from home, Tapio has a variety of different needs from his broadband and his mobile service provider. He needs primarily to be able to check email, store contacts and easily upload and download files through secure networks. His wife would also need a good home internet connection for her own home/office lifestyle having even more need for the ability to upload and download large files. He is in the market for his own broadband connection and mobile phone contract.

Products: Broadband Internet Connection; Mobile phone contract. Meet Tapio........

Goals	Purchase broadband connection for home use
Scena -rio	Tapio has decided he needs to get a broadband connection for his own personal home use. He has just moved apartment and needs a new service. He and his wife

	both know through word of mouth that they are in a buyers market and will use the internet to find the best deal they can. Also through word of mouth Tapio heard technical details that 100Mb was a fast broadband connection. Tapio knows all the major brands via offline branding campaigns such as TV, billboards and stickers on the sides of public transport vehicles.
Tasks prior to pur- chase	Check brand websites directly. Compare brand prices (Google). Compare full service offers (Google). Figure out if 100Mb is what he needs to run a good connection from home Learn how to install the system
Consid- erations and question s	The are a variety of broadband deals in Finland so it is important to find out what the brands offer. • What is the price per month? • How many service/price (speed to Mb ratio) options are there and are they understandable? • Does the cost vary based on usage? If so how? If not is the price fixed or could there be hidden surprises? • Tapios wife doesn't want to use cables to connect to the Internet. Is

	the broadband connection wireless? Does this cost more?
	• Do any free accessories (ie wireless modem) come with the service?
	• Are there any free offers in Finland around broadband?
	• If so are the free offers comparable in terms of features?
	• Tapio heard that a full system contract including digital TV could be purchased with broadband access to the Internet? Is this possible in his location?
	• Does the system come home-fitted? Is it manual installation? If so is it easy?
	• Are there service guarantees? Money back options or trial periods?
Pain points	Neither Tapio nor his wife have any idea how to install broadband and don't know anything about the technology. Tapio heard he needed a 100Mb connection because it's fast but doesn't know how much benefit he will get for the extra money.
Search terms	Finnish terms (same in English); Laajakaista (broadband) Laajakaista Yhteys (broadband connection)

	Laajakaista Nopeus (broadband fast/speed) Laajakaista Hinnat (broadband prices)
Key paths/ content	Look on the website that Tapio will use for the information that answers all his considerations/questions. Reproduced by kind permission of Steve Jackson, Cult of Analytics

Personas are important. They ensure your web site, content marketing, ads etc. are written to help real specific people in real specific situations. You can see more on developing personas in appendix 1.

Scenario Planning

Scenario planning identifies different scenarios that personas may have while using the product or service. While Personas describe typical users (and their needs, goals, and motivations), Scenario Planning describes the actual usage (or event/s) while using that product, service or website. There may be several scenarios as in the case of a chocolate company's website which might have visitors who want chocolates for a wedding, other visitors want to express their love and others may want the chocolates for a dinner party (3 different scenarios). Scenario planning helps marketers to 'ground the designers in the world inhabited by the user' (Erlhoff and Marshall, 2008). You can see arguably, the best ever example of scenario planning, by National Semiconductor (who makes

B2B chips for mobiles and DVD players) in appendix 2. Their scenario planning actually created sustainable competitive advantage.

Who are your visitors?

You can see your visitor profiles from your analytics package. This information is automatically collected (and freely available from say Google Analytics). This tells you what percentage of your visitors come from which locations and via which devices. Some analytics now also guesstimate the gender and age of your visitors. Google also reveals, in aggregate, what these visitors are interested in (see 'Why' later). Similarly, Facbook insights gives aggregate data on age, gender, location and interests of your visitors/fans as well as which content generates most engagement.

What are their interests and stage in the buying process?

Although this question helps to build a profile (describing who your visitors are), it also overlaps with the 'Why' question as their click behaviour (what they click on and the duration they spend on it) leaves a trail of their interests, what engaged them and what didn't. Click behaviour is also called 'digital body language'. Either way, an individual's interest and stage in the buying process can be recorded (see KPMG example, Appendix 3) and also, the aggregate behaviour can be recorded i.e. how many visitors were interested in certain products or pages. Some data service companies offer to layer on an individual's interests which are taken from publicly available social media 'interests' declared.

Identifying what buying stage a visitor is at via key Phrases

Keywords used in a search engine can indicate how advanced a potential customer is in their online buying journey. People searching with specific key phrases self- categorise themselves into a particular stage of the buying process. For example, searchers using the following key phrases:

- "electric adjustable beds" could still be in the **research phase**

- "electric adjustable beds reviews" – getting close to being **ready to buy**.

- "buy electric adjustable beds" - likely looking to **make a purchase** soon.

You can find actual terms and volumes using Google's Keyword Planner. You do have to set up with Google AdWords, but use of the tool is free. It's essential if you're interested in learning more about your customers.

1. Research Phase

It's worth remembering that your potential customer may only be aware of their pain, not the solution. However, focusing on prospects who seek a solution and are in the initial research phase of their buying journey, the initial keywords they start searching with might include:

Electric adjustable bed, electric adjustable bed tips, electric adjustable bed help, electric adjustable bed advice, best electric adjustable bed, cheap electric adjustable beds.

2. Advanced Phase

These prospects have done some research. They know what they want, and now need to create a 'considered set' of just a few brands that they like. They may also be interested in finding the best quality for the least money. At this point, they are **looking for reviews and comparison shopping**. Keywords or phrases indicating this stage of the buying journey might be:

'electric adjustable bed reviews'

'compare [your brand name] with [your competitor brand name]'

3. Buy Phase

At the final stages of a sometimes a tortuous journey, these buyers are very focused and ready to buy. They'll be using these kinds of phrases:

'buy electric adjustable bed'

'purchase electric adjustable bed'

'get electric adjustable bed'

'electric adjustable bed signup'

'contact electric adjustable bed'

They want an easy, convenient, clearly sign-posted route to buy (with options – some want to buy over the phone, others in person and others prefer the website.) Therefore they need easy to find information, contact details, phone numbers, references and proof of quality.

Want to get potential customers from your competitor?

Try '[Keyword] coupon' in a Pay Per Click ad. Generally, people search for this term when they're ready to buy. Offer your lead a discount that's automatically added to their cart/signup (and make the checkout process simple), so they go through you and not the competition. (Tiffany da Silva, 2014)

Now have a look at how KPMG, one of the world's top four professional services firms identify 'Who Is Their B2B Visitor' (and the visitor's possible needs from their click behaviour). They categorise/segment visitors into 'Visit Type' according to their click behaviour which is based on 'how the visit originates, how it ends and/or what happened during the visit'.

Here are 14 categories (or segments) that KPMG use to classify who each visitor is according to their on-site behaviour (i.e. their click behaviour):

- Prospect (submits an Request For a Proposal [RFP] or an email to a partner)
- Participant (registers for an event, the site or content)
- Passive Browser (downloads single articles, papers, starts but doesn't finish a video)

- Researcher (downloads multiple articles, papers, starts and completes more than one video in multiple practice areas or industries)
- Advocate (reads an article or paper, or views a video and shares it)
- Focused Seeker (reads multiple content items within a practice area or industry)
- Passive Job Seeker (reads content on the Jobs Section of the site)
- Engaged Job Seeker (submits a job search query and views job details)
- Participating Job Seeker (submits their résumé)
- Brand Aware Visitor – First Time and Repeat (a visitor that comes to the site directly)
- Responder (responds to a KPMG email campaign, or clicks on a link within an alert or newsletter)
- Brand Aware Searcher (comes to KPMG website through branded SEO, PPC, display ads on third party sites)
- Non-Brand Aware Searcher (comes to KPMG website through non-branded SEO or PPC)
- Passive Social Visitor (comes from a social media property (Facbook, Twitter, YouTube) one time)
- Engaged Social Visitor (comes from a social media property (Facbook, Twitter, YouTube) and conducts one of the Engagement actions described in the Metrics Taxonomy)

You can see this in more detail in a table in appendix 3.

What are their names, jobs and addresses – registration data?

You can, of course, ask your visitors to register and tell you who they are, and in return you can give them some content that is relevant to their needs. People will not give up personal information unless there is a personal benefit to them. Remember you can only collect limited individual profile information and names via registration. I say 'limited' as it's best not to ask for too much information too early as it annoys customers and reduces conversion rates. HSBC conversion rates increased by 2,000% by reducing the number of questions from 17 to 4 questions. See the Action section for more.

What are their names, addresses and interests – reverse forensics?

Some visitor analysis companies use 'reverse forensics' to identify approximately 20% of the visitors to a B2B website by identifying the visitor's IP address, url , company name, location, general contact details (including general telephone number), what page(s) each visitor was interested in (and duration), what phrases they used when searching and now you can pair that data up with another services company such as CrowdVu.com to find actual people in specific job titles (telephone number, email address and social information).

Additional customer information from progressive profiling

You can continually add information about customers and prospects from, firstly, each interaction on the website, and secondly, from different sources both online and offline. If you have an integrated database and the automated processes you can continually upload relevant information to ultimately build a better visitor profile. So each click on a website and combined with public profile information on various social platforms, layered with other public databases can build an even more detailed profile of your customers.

'Tying customer behavioural data from all online and offline sources
with past purchase and customer service history
to segment and communicate with the buyer
in a personalized fashion
previously only dreamed of.'
(Eloqua, 2013)

Who are your followers?

Who are your Twitter followers?
You can see where your Twitter followers come from and how influential they are (Who) and when they go online (How) by using Followerwonk.com (or similar services).

Who are your Facbook followers?
Facbook Insights gives free analytics which reveal the demographic breakdown of your fans followers and also which time and type of content generates more engagement.

Who are your LinkedIn followers?

Your LinkedIn Company Page gives you free Follower Analytics which reveals your followers' demographics and sources, which content gets read and how you compare to competition (see the 1 min video called 'Get Insights with Company Page Analytics' from Linkedin Marketing Solutions on Youtube).

Who are your influential customers and visitors/followers?

Who are the influencers that spread your content? How many do they reach? What content was received well? Knowing who's interested in what you have to say helps you to get to know them and ensure they always see your content. Here's some services that identify your influencers and what interests them:

- Crowdbooster.com identifies who is influential that shares your content.
- Newsle.com alerts you whenever any of your LinkedIn connections are in the press.
- BuzzSumo is another free tool that identifies influencers (it also identifies content that's performing really well under different keywords and phrases).
- Klout identifies how influential tweeters are by giving them a Klout score. Followerwonk identifies location, language, gender and influence of your Twitter followers and also helps measure yourself against competitors audit and track followers.
- Google's Referral Analysis (Google Analytics) shows you who is linking to you and referring traffic to you and which referral sources get

you the most traffic and are the most influential.
- CrowdVu identifies any influencers automatically once you insert a key phrase, brand or company; it identifies who is talking about it and, most importantly, who are the most influential ones.*

CrowdVu can also find who are your B2B Influencers according to their level of influence, segmenting based on location, industry, company name, conversations, hashtags or any other business field e.g. 'Find me "influential Twitter users, who are based in London and who work at companies in the finance industry where their revenue is greater than £200 million per year".'

> 'There's too much talking in social media and not enough listening and learning.'
> (Brian Solis, 2012)
> TEDTalk: Reinventing Consumer Capitalism – Screw Business as Usual

Who is talking about your product (or your type of product)?

Here are seven ways to find out who is talking about you and what they are saying:
(taken from The Old Marketing Ship Is Sinking on www.PRSmith.org/blog):

1. Listen to customer service

2. Listen to customer feedback:
   Reevoo, Feefo and Trust Pilot

3. Listen To Customer Communities:
   GetSatisfaction, UserVoice, UserEcho andMer
   echo.com

Photo courtesy of hubspot

4. Listen to local chatter (Twitter), Twitter
   search's 'advanced search' (see box) and
   listening To Mentions and Messages on
   Twitter via TweetDeck, Hootsuite,
   SocialBro, TweetReach, Tweriod and Twilert.

5. Listen to multiple websites (feed readers).

6. Listen to influencers: newslee.com alerts you
   when your LinkedIn connections are in the
   press. Followerwonk identifies demographics
   and influence

location, language, and gender of your Twitter followers and also helps measure yourself against competitors audit and track followers; Google Alerts (now called GigaAlert) and CrowdVu and mention.net .

7. Listen to the mood of the market – Sentiment Analysis.

Social Mention (blogs, comments, bookmarks, events, news, videos), TwitterSearch: search by topic, people, hashtags, words, exact phrase, 'near this place', BoardReader (forums and boards), Google Blog Search, WhosTalkin.com (mostly free). There are some paid-for tools that summarise all the conversationsand deliver a single sentiment score as well as allowing you to drill down and engage in those conversations namely Radian6, Alterian (now called SM2), SysomosMAP and Brandwatch.

Who Is Talking About Your Product Type via Twitter's Advance Search?

Using Twitter's standard search engine you can find people talking about a certain topic (#topic), companies, brands or people or even tweets from particular people. You can narrow your search to a specific region or to people who are looking for your product (brand or general category) in a specific area, or who are talking about a competitor. Twitter advanced search can do this for you and a lot more. See Action section for more.

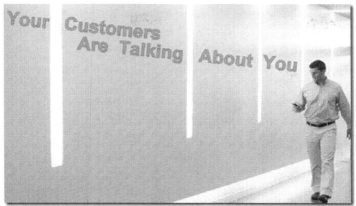

Photo courtesy: Hubspot and PR Smith

Who is attending a particular conference or event?

We can generate databases of people who attend a particular conference or event, what they say about certain topics and contact details, once they tweet comments with the conference/event hashtag. See Tactics for more on this.

Ask your data and you shall receive

Data can be integrated analysed and used in so many new ways. Your ability to ask good questions, may determine your future success. See how you can search data for new customer profiles in the Tactics section.

**Your (Facbook) likes can reveal
your sexuality, race, drug use and your parents'
divorce**

Individuals can be analysed on Facbook to reveal a lot more about an individual. For example, new analytics software from Microsoft and Cambridge University (tested on 58,000 volunteers) analyses and identifies a person's private and very sensitive personal attributes based on their Facbook 'ikes' such as your sexual orientation, drug use, religious and political views, intelligence, happiness, age, gender and more. Could your 'likes' be analysed before a job interview or a major negotiation? (Cambridge University and Microsoft, 2013)

Your Tweets linguistic footprint reveals your real personality

IBM's Twitter psycholinguistics (analysis of anyone's choice of words when using Twitter) can 'reveal an individual's personality traits from just 200 of your tweets in 20 seconds' (Takahashi, 2013).

Extracting correlations between a person's word choice (and activity patterns) can reveal these intrinsic traits as dutiful, conscientious, conservative, introvert.

These 'linguistic footprints' (in the public domain) can now replace (or enhance) the old segmentation variables. They can also identify if you are happy or depressed (different words used).

It's not surprising then to hear that WPP, the world's largest communications group, has entered into a long term contract with Twitter.

Profiling customers during a routine customer service call

'Yet technology can decipher signals that we aren't even aware of. Mattersight is a company that has developed software that can analyze your personality during a routine customer service call. In his book, Honest Signals, MIT's Sandy Pentland describes a machine that can predict behavior from subtle physical cues.'   (Satell, 2014)

See an organisation's previous websites

'The Way Back Machine' (now called the 'Internet Archive') reveals all previous versions of a website which, in turn, reveals how a company is changing (e.g. mission statements, Unique Selling Points, Online Value Propositions, size of team/staff, old product ranges and more). Useful when doing a sales pitch, or proposing a strategic alliance or even before a job interview.

Who is in an organisation's staff?

LinkedIn Advanced Search lets you insert a company name to see how many people work there (or in a particular department), how many are in your network, or you can search by location or industry type. If you are in B2B, you can even learn about prospective customers with company size (employees), Fortune 500 companies closest to your network (first degree or second degree contacts), and even companies hiring.

See the 4 minute TweetDeck video called 'Tweetdeck Search' by Traci Knoppe on Youtube.

Once you know the ideal customer profile you can find new customers
The Tactics section will briefly explore how new databases, new ad networks, and new targeting tools can be exploited, once you know who is your ideal customer. For now, let's move onto the second big customer question, 'Why?'

1.1.2 Why?

Why do customers buy or not buy from you? Why do they visit or not visit your site? Why do they come back a second time to your site? Why do other visitors leave or 'bounce' after less than 30 seconds? 'Why' is the most difficult of the 'Who, Why and How' questions. Sometimes this is because customers themselves, don't fully know why they buy.

The good news is that, in addition to the traditional offline market research techniques, there is a plethora of new online tools (many of them are free) which help to answer this, sometimes complex, 'Why' question.

Without knowing the answer to the 'why' question, marketers waste resources by offering the wrong proposition. For example, the multi-billion dollar football business, doesn't know why their customers (fans) buy their services. Many football businesses will not survive, in fact, most football clubs in the UK are losing money constantly – despite having customer loyalty levels that most marketers can only dream of having.

> ## Most marketers don't fully know what their visitors' interests are
> Only 45% of marketers are capturing and consolidating customer behavioural data from multiple channels in a single database.
> (Silverpop/Forrester, 2013)

There is a great online opportunity to get customer insights that were never previously available freely and quickly. Many businesses combine offline focus groups and surveys with online insights (discussions, analytics and surveys). These customer insights can be fascinating – whoever imagined that customers would have a 'relationship with a tin of paint' (read on).

> ## A relationship with a tin of paint
> People walk in and choose Dulux paint. They don't know why they choose Dulux paint. It might be to do with the shaggy dogs in the ads, but it is a sad fact there are human beings in our country who have a relationship with a tin of paint.
> (Laurie Young, 2014)

'Why?' is a difficult question, e.g. why do football fans watch football?
A few years ago I asked these football fans 'why do you buy tickets to the games?' They didn't actually

know the real reason! So they couldn't tell me. None of them mention 'football' or 'to see a football match'. It is extraordinary. It is also true. Watch the video.

See Man Utd fans talk about why they buy on Youtube PRSmith1000

If using Maslow's Hierarchy of Needs it seems that football satisfies middle level needs ('to be loved').

Not happy with these answers, I took a camera crew to Harvard Business School to interview the late, great Professor Ted Levitt.

Professor Levitt suggested that fans going to football, or ice hockey, or a rock concert enjoyed 'a transcendental affair' (higher level Maslow needs being satisfied).

Subtle stuff, but I am convinced that he was correct.

Most UK football clubs lose money – possibly because they don't fully understand why their customers buy, i.e. possibly they don't understand that they are selling a 'transcendental affair' to both the fans inside the ground and the millions around the globe who seek:
'unconscious relationships and transcendental experiences' via football?

See Harvard's Professor Ted Levitt onYoutube PRSmith1000

Finding the answer to why customers buy is not easy. Offline questions/discussions and even surveys can sometimes struggle to extract the real reason. However online digital body language based on actual customer behaviour (including what phrases they use to find the site) does not lie. Web analytics don't lie. Now let's explore the complex 'why' question.

So here are some of the 'Why' questions we are going to consider:

- What are your customers' needs? What do they really want?
- What do your customers like (or dislike) about your product/service?
- What are your customers' future needs?
- What are your visitor's needs and what are they interested in?
- Why do your visitors return to some sites and not to others?
- Why do your visitors not convert?
- What marketing content do your visitors specifically like?

- What marketing content do your influencers like?
- What part of your content (e.g. a webinar) does your audience like?
- What is being said about you (or your product type) locally? What's trending?

What are your customer needs?

In addition to listening to customer service feedback, use customer reviews and traditional offline market research to ask customers what they want and what their preferences are, you can see customer needs expressed via the phrases they use in search engines (on your site and outside your site).

This is valuable information as its customers are succinctly describing their needs in their words (not yours). Once you understand customer needs you can then work backwards. Read on.

Determine your customers' need and work backwards

'Specs for Amazon's big new projects such as its Kindle tablets and e-book readers have been defined by customers' desires rather than engineers' tastes. If customers don't want something it's gone, even if that means breaking apart a once powerful department.' Rule no. 5 of Amazon boss, Jeff Bezos's 10 Leadership Lessons (Anders, 2012)

What are your visitor's needs and what are they interested in?

Identifying key phrases (used to search for your product or service) and 'click behaviour' (number of pages, visits and average duration) reveals what your visitors are interested in. Although Google has recently made it more difficult to see these key phrases you can link Google Web Master tools with Google Analytics to identify key phrases (See SmartInsights.com's Web Master Tools and SEO Effectiveness for more.).

Ask visitors 'What did you come to our site today to do?' via an on-site survey.

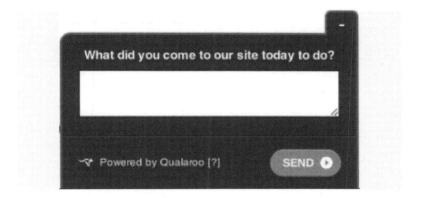

Competitive advantage from integrating Twitter data with analytics
Twitter's brand insights and customer research are powerful. It provides 'a window into consumer attitudes and behaviour in real time' says Martin Sorrel, CEO of the world's biggest marketing

communications services, WPP. So when the group says that two thirds of the benefits of Twitter are Analysis and Analysis (brand insights and customer research) and then signs a global partnership agreement with Twitter, it makes you stop and think. The global strategy allows the comms giant to gain competitive advantage by integrating Twitter data into its media and analytics platforms (Ibrahim, 2013).

Follow the conversations - Get Alerts About What Customers/Markets Want

It's worth mentioning some of these tools again: GigaAlert (formerly Google Alert) for alerts about any topic by journalists and major bloggers; CrowdVu,com covers who is discussing what and how influential they are and where they are based; Newslee.com alerts you whenever any of your influential LinkedIn connections are in the media; Followerwonk.com identifies who your Twitter followers are; news readers like feedly.com monitor several blogs; Sentiment Analysis actually summarises all conversations and puts a score on the sentiment or mood which reflects what's being said about a brand. It also allows you to drill down, see who is saying what and with the option of respondoning.

Why does your community exist?

If you have a community, you need to be crystal clear why it exists. Understanding why your community exists and why customers like your community is fundamental to your future growth. You'll be pleasantly surprised to learn that it is not always about discounts.

What do your customers like (or dislike) about your product/service?

Useful customer feedback comes from product review services like Reevoo, Feefo and Trust Pilot who track down customers and get product reviews. Customer Communities like:
- GetSatisfaction
- Uservoice
- UserEcho

discuss products and services and reveal what customers like and dislike. Some brands even own their own customer panels (see NASCAR example).

Biggest sport uses fan councils

The world's biggest spectator sport NASCAR combines online listening tools, including online official NASCAR Fan Council (customer panel) to gather information about what the fans like and don't like about the user experience online and offline.

In addition Website Pop Up Surveys can ask a few short questions about what customers like or dislike and more general online discussions can be monitored for comments about, and mentions, of your products (and your competitors' products) via social listening tools already mentioned (and also discussed on www.PRSmith.org/blog).

What are your customers' future needs?

Can you anticipate your customer's future needs? Yes, RFM, Customer Life Cycles, Collaborative Filtering, Time/Date/Event/purchase triggers and social media likes can all indicate a customer's likelihood of purchasing. Here's a brief description of each. See Tactics for more.

Future needs: RFM

A customer's Recency, Frequency and Monetary spending is a useful predictor of the probability of them continuing to purchase. See Tactics for more.

Future needs: customer life cycle

Many companies measure a customer's LTV (Life Time Value) since if they deliver a great service, they can retain a customer for their buying life. And it's possible to predict when they are ready to purchase again. See Tactics for more.

Future needs: time triggered, date triggered, event triggered and purchase triggered

Time may trigger a purchase such as six months after a car is bought it needs its first service. Date triggered events like birthdays or Father's Day triggers more buying and purchase triggered means buying product A means you will also need product B.

Future needs: collaborative filtering

Collaborative filtering makes intelligent guesses at what else a buyer might like to buy e.g. when you buy a book from Amazon they check to see what other books buyers of this publication have also bought. They then offer these highly relevant additional books to you.

Future needs: Facbook likes increase propensity to purchase

There is a logical correlation between 'liking' a brand on Facbook and an increased propensity to purchase. So a highly engaging Facbook activity could support an increase in sales. See Tactics on whether to increase spending on Facbook.

Anticipating future demand for new music via deep twitter analysis

Music is the most popular topic on Twitter. Although there were 1B+ tweets about music last year, this gold mine of data has not yet been mined. Twitter data is much sought after – CNN are partnering with Twitter to develop a news alert for journalists. Music company, 300, is partnering to scan for excitement about new bands (particularly from influencers) and then get alerts. 300 now has access to Twitter's data pile, including information not in the public domain such as the location tags that identify from where a tweet was sent. "The goal, is to mine Twitter for the kind of signs that music scouts have always sought, like a flicker of excitement about a fledgling band" said Lyor Cohen. (Sisario, 2014).

Why do your visitors return to some sites and not to others?

Jacob Nielsen's original research into why visitors come back a second time revealed the same four key factors year after year. The percentages vary each year but the same four satisfaction factors pop up every year:

- Relevant Content
- Easy Navigation
- Quick Download
- Fresh Content

Does your website satisfy your visitors?
Find out. Ask your visitors. You can use a short pop up satisfaction survey. Or at the very least, you must do some Usability Testing' to ensure your website is fully functional and easy to use. The Control section explores these in more detail.

Why do your visitors not convert?

Why do, say, only 1%, of your visitors convert (e.g. download a white paper, register for a newsletter or take a trial or buy)?

It could be a combination of attracting the wrong type of visitor or they are unable to convert because your site makes it too difficult for them. You can compare your conversion rate with others.

Also see the Control section for more.

Incidentally, if you assign money values to goals or Ecommerce tracking is set up, you can also see how each page assists in conversion (through the Google Analytics Page Value metric).

What marketing content do your visitors specifically like?

Analytics packages like Google Analytics reveal which products (specific pages) are most popular (number of visits and duration). Most analytics packages reveal which content gets the most engagement. Site customer feedback surveys also tell us more about visitor needs – particularly 'unmet needs' i.e. what else they'd like to see.

What marketing content do your influencers like?

Referral data reveals which people, or sites, link to which pages on your site (i.e. which of your pages appeal to other website owners). This tells you firstly, who is linking to you and secondly, gives you some clues about what content to focus on creating.

Note: referral data is available through several sources, for example, Google Analytics or other analytics systems. Google Webmaster Tools shows you what specific content external sites (or bloggers or influencers) link to. You can also monitor which of your tweets get retweeted by influencers, for example, we use Hootsuite.

Observe influencers

See what their most popular posts are. See what questions they ask on different social platforms. Engage in their discussions. Eventually ask these influencers what content or topics they might like to see. Or perhaps, if they might like to see a sneak preview of certain content.

You can constantly improve by asking customers (and prospects) great questions -even granular ones such as 'which part of a webinar did you enjoy most?' You need to prioritise your questions and not ask customers for too much of their time.

What part of your content (e.g. a webinar) does your audience like?

You can ask your audiences to do a 1 minute post webinar survey to analyse what your visitors actually enjoyed about the webinar, such as the presenter, the presentation, the topic (i.e. 'why they liked it?') and if there are additional topics they'd like to know about.

Why do people share things?
We share things to build our own personal brand and look good online.

What is being said about you locally?

You can listen to conversations taking place near you (geographically e.g. within a 25km radius of where you are, or within a certain country).

Twithawk and Twitter Advanced Search can find people talking in real time about your chosen topic, listen to them and, if you choose, easily engage with your audience mid-conversation.

> ## Most customers talk about you rather than with you
> Only 9% of tweets mentioning companies start with @ which means 91% of people are talking about you, not to you. (Radcliff, 2014)

Understanding customer needs in the future - emotion recognition

Future communications systems will detect a customer's mood and tailor responses accordingly. Emotion recognition (detected by voice if using voice operated software or by your choice of words used in search engine or Tweet or a Facbook post). Face recognition and good old body language recognition may follow. Essentially, 'context is king', hence tailored responses that are relevant to your mood, your company, your device, your location, and your past history will achieve better response levels. Also recognising a customer's device, location (and time of activity) reveals different types of needs a customer might have. Tailored responses will be more relevant and therefore get better responses.

Facbook can predict when you are going to change a relationship

Recent attempts by Facbook's data science team shows the incredible power of analyzing data. For example, Facbook revealed that it can now safely predict when a user is about to change their relationship status from 'single' to 'in a relationship'. The insights come from analyzing the way we exchange messages and post on our timeline just before we 'commit'.

The question is, what else will Facbook be able to predict? (Marr 2014). Sophisticated predictive analytics teams have been around for years (Duhigg 2012).

What's trending?

Sites like Google Trends and Trendsmap.com let you see what's trending in different places. Who is speaking and what is being spoken about in different regions around the world. This can also be useful for small local business owners who may have a small, community-led audience, as it will allow them to identify the key topics in that local area and to weave these topics into their marketing efforts. Google Zeitgeist was the annual Zeitgeist report (up to 2012) revealing what captured the world's attention in the preceding year - our passions, interests and defining moments as seen through search.

**Future trend
– online and offline all the same**

"The superficial line between the offline and the online will eventually disappear as wearable technology and connected smart devices become the norm"
(Anders Sorman-Nilsson, 2014) in an interview with Muireann Bolger, Digital Disruption, The Marketer

---

So it's not surprising that the 'Why?' question is the most difficult question to answer. It requires a deep understanding of your customer's psyche. Some offline tools help us to gather some customer insights and many new online tools help us to find answers to the final question 'How – do customers buy?'

Why we do what we do

What do people really want?
Unique - people want to feel unique.
Connectedness – yet people want to feel connected to others.
Paradoxically, we also need to feel we belong, that we are not alone in the world and that we are part of something larger. (Adams, 2014)
Do you agree or disagree?

1.1.3 How?

So we've looked at 'Who' and 'Why', now consider, 'How'. By this, I mean two things: how do your customers actually buy (what are their processes/steps or journey), and how do they process information? How do customers make their decisions? How do they discover your site? By what route (or what was their digital journey)? Did they move between online and offline? Which particular digital channels get the best visitors (i.e. traffic that converts towards a goal)? Channels include advertising (PPC and banner ads), social media, direct mail, referral links, (using your web url).

Here are some questions which we can now answer using analytics:

- How do customers buy (what is their online journey)?
- How long and how many channels do your visitors use?
- What stage are your visitors at in the buying process?
- How many pages are ideal during a visit?
- When is the best time to post content and engage?
- How do your customers process information?
- How do customers prefer to view initial information?
- How do customers perceive your website?
- How do some videos work better than others?
- How do some words work better than others?
- What percentage of your visitors view your site on a mobile?
- How do customers see things differently on their mobile?

How do customers buy - what is their online journey?

Customers generally make more than one visit to a site before buying. Their multiple visits also often come from many different channels whether a general organic search (via a search engine) or a branded search, a PPC ad, a link or by directly inserting the web address into a browser. Just like in football it is often the last pass, or assist, that is as important as the scorer of the goal (or the last channel in this case). So we need to know which route generates the most conversions (or sales). Google's Multi-Channel Funnel Analysis does this (you'll find several videos on youtube).

Analytics packages answer almost all of these questions. As long as you add some Google Analytics code to each page of your website and tag all your email and ad campaigns (add a tiny bit of code which can be automatically added by marketing services), then you can access all of these reports and see which routes (or customer journeys) deliver the best conversions (within the last 2 months). Remember 'conversions' are predefined goals, such as moving a visitor onto a specific page; signing up for a newsletter; a free sample; a trial period, or even making a purchase. More on Google Analytics and tracking campaigns in SmartInsights.com.

You can even filter via campaign or keywords to see what's working by using Google Analytics Multi-Channel Funnel Analysis (Keyword Assisted - Assisted Conversions Report) so that you can invest more in what's working and stop what's not working. Continually analysing these visitor journeys helps marketers to continually optimise their returns on investment.

How long and how many channels do your visitors use?

The Path Length Report reveals how long (in days and in interactions) it takes for visitors to become customers. The Top Path Conversion Path Reports reveals the paths visitors took on their way to converting to a customer, the number of conversions from each path, and the value of those conversions. In other words, this in turn, reveals which channels generate (or even just assist) more conversions than others?

Which channels do your customers use the most?

Social channel identification tools identify where your target audience are communicating about your brand, your competitors and other relevant topics, i.e. if most of your customers' discussions are on LinkedIn and not Twitter, you should invest more resource on LinkedIn groups, advertising etc. See Tactics for more.

What stage are your visitors at in the buying process?

As mentioned in the 'Who' questions, click behaviour leaves a trail of visitor interests - what they clicked on (what engaged them). This is digital body language. It also reveals how advanced a visitor is in the buying process. Also as a rough rule of thumb the longer the search term indicates the further the customer is in the buying process/journey.

When is the best time to post content and Engage?

As abhorrent as it may seem, not everyone is on Twitter 24/7. So it's best to tweet when they are firstly, online andsecondly, on Twitter.
Tweriod identifies the best times for you to tweet by analysing both your tweets and your followers' tweets to help you tweet at the best time. Other analytical tools identify when is the best time to post on Facbook and other platforms.

When is the best time to send an email?

Email newsletter platforms like Mailchimp analysed over one billion emails to discover that after 12pm and in particular between 2-5pm on Thursdays were the best time to send an email. Use analytics to determine when is the best time for you – this will increase your open rates and conversion rates. Another American analysis from WebMarketingToday suggests Fridays, Saturdays and Sundays were best as busy people catch up with their emails over the weekend.

It really does depend on your industry as travel businesses often say Monday is the best day (when people need a lift!) You've simply got to test your emails in a disciplined way and you will learn exactly when is best to send and to post. Nearly all email platforms have their own customer insights or analytics which tell you, (amongst other really useful information) when is the best time to post content.

How do your customers process information?

We need to know how customers look at our website, our email shots, our ads etc. Do they see the key things we want them to see? How do they process information?
In small chunks, is the answer. Customers process small chunks of information initially.

How do customers prefer to view initial information?

We are drawn to visual media. We have less time, shorter attention spans and more distractions as we multitask.

The shift towards visual and social
Picture paints 1000 words

Blogs have 500-1000 (or more) words
Facbook has just a few words*
Twitter: 140 characters**
Youtube: no words***
Vine: 6s video - ditto
Pinterest: no words
Instagram: ditto

*Facbook posts with pictures and videos get more engagement
** Tweets with pictures get more engagement
*** well, very few words – just some in the title, caption, credits and description
(and the full transcript plus annotations can also now be included)

Adapted from Joe Dalton (2012)

See also 6 Tips to exploit this visual opportunity in chapter 5, Action.

So perception is a delicate and highly biased variable. Just because you have made the most beautiful website, Facbook page, Instagram photos, ad, email or virtual event, doesn't necessarily mean the customer will also see it as beautiful. Customers may not be able to see it, read it, click it or use it because they don't see what you want them to see. Therefore we have to test everything.

Shrinking attention spans

The world's first televised presidential debate was between Nixon and Kennedy in 1960. Harvard University predicted that the average attention span was 42 seconds. Kennedy responded in 40 second site bites. JFK won.

In 2008 attention span had dropped to less than 5 seconds. 'Yes We Can' seemed to fit the time available! Obama also won the 2012 race.

Why do you like reading these vignettes?

These invaluable customer insights about how Americans process information helped the Obama campaign to deliver the right message in the right way so that the audience could more easily process it.

This is the Magic Marketing formula at its best:
- identify needs
- reflect them
- deliver a reasonable product

You can see President Obama's head of digital, Teddy Goff, discussing with me how they used customer insights (particularly behavioural insights) and big data to deliver a winning campaign on my unoffical Youtube site 'PR Smith'.

NB this is different to my main PRSmith1000 youtube site.

How audiences process and use social media – See President Obama's Head of Digital, Teddy Goff in conversation with PR Smith in Dublin's, Lansdowne Road, international rugby venue

How do customers perceive your website?

Session Maps and Heat Maps (see next page) are used to try to understand how customers process information on a website.

Session Maps record an individual's eye movements across a web page (erratic/random eye movement suggests confusion).

The larger the circle the more time spent looking.

Session Map courtesy of www.etre.com

The results of all the individual Session Maps are then aggregated to generate a single Heat Map (see next page) with warmer colours revealing areas most looked at and 'black' indicating no one looked at this part of the page (in this case no one noticed the 'Sale' sign).

Heat Map courtesy of www.etre.com

That's probably why most organisations put their brand top left. Incidentally the eye movement used to be an 'F', starting top left , scanning across, reverting to top left and then scanning down and across (to complete the top two rows of the 'F').

Usability testing is different. Basically it asks customers (and other stakeholders) to use the website to carry out specific tasks and an observer watches how easy or difficult it is to complete the tasks. See the Control section for more.

How do some videos work better than others?

Why do some videos work better than others? Which bits of your videos arouse emotion? For ads, virals, demos? Live research is conducted by some companies who deliver Emotional Response Video Analysis. Basically they have recruited audiences ready and waiting to watch your videos. Their reaction (including body language/facial reaction and even pupil dilation) identifies which parts of your video arouse customers and which bits don't.

This helps video makers to cut out the bland content and release the high impact video clips which increases the likelihood of the videos being liked, discussed and shared.

How do some words work better than others?

Changing a single word on a website has resulted in a 300% increase in click through rate – Microsoft once claimed.

There is no doubt that certain words trigger far better reactions than others. Constant Beta testing key phrases and data analysis helps.

Which worked best?

President Obama's Digital Director, Teddy Goff, told me that one of these statements had a much higher impact than the other:

- 'you should be a donor'

- 'you should donate'

Which one, do you think, worked best during the last Obama campaign?

Stop and think for a moment before reading the answer. Teddy Goff discovered that people were more likely to be persuaded by the first statement as nouns were found to be more powerful than verbs (Lee, 2013). Sometimes we just don't fully know why this is, but testing and analysis will reveal which works best. Hence the importance of developing a constant beta culture. Do check out how changing one button on a website boosted revenues so much that they named it The $300 Million Button (just Google it).

Perception of same images differ between consumers and producers
- the chasm between 'fully human' and 'nearly human'

In the 1970s, Japanese robotics engineer, Masahiro Mori, observed that the more human his robots appeared, the more people reacted positively towards them. But when robots look too similar to humans (but still seen as a robot) people saw them as **'visually revolting'**. Mori called this 'The Uncanny Valley' – the chasm between 'fully human' and 'nearly human'. More recently audiences didn't like the very realistic looking Final Fantasy movie animation (some children cried). Was this the 'Uncanny Valley'? Dreamworks Studios were aware of this when producing Shrek particularly when they tested their product (test screenings). They discovered that children perceived the movie to be spooky because the animations were almost real. Dreamworks then changed the characters to be less real and more cartoon-like.

Do customers see things differently on their mobile?

What percentage of your visitors view your site on a mobile?

You will find this figure is growing every year. But even if it is as low as 10%, that's 10% of all of your visitors to whom you are delivering a bad user experience as their clumsy big thumbs try to click tiny tabs, and tediously expanding screens with cumbersome double fingers is rapidly becoming too time consuming and too inconvenient. All the analytics packages (Google, Facbook etc) will tell you what percentage are accessing your online platforms via which devices.

What percentage of your customers read emails on a mobile?

What device do your customers read their emails with? A 2013 Marketing Sherpa Mobile Marketing Benchmark Report revealed that 31% of email marketers do not know their mobile email open rate. You need to think about the content you use. Is the content mobile-friendly? Are the Calls To Action clearly visible and easily clickable on a small screen?

Do customers process information differently on mobile?

The UX (User Experience) on the mobile is unique as users process information differently when they are on their mobiles because they are often multi-tasking, more likely to be interrupted and the small screen size means that reading comprehension plummets. See appendix 4 for this excellent piece:

'Marketing on Mobile: Why is this Platform Different?' by Goldberg, 2013.

Mobile
Think more about 'mobility' as opposed to 'mobile'. Think about: what they see on your website landing page, or how your email looks on their small screen; the state of mind of the user and how their environment is different to sitting in an office.

Let's wrap up this 'How' question with 10 Great 'How' Questions from Steve Jackson (2009) Cult of Analytics. Can you answer all of these?

10 great 'HOW' questions
1. What are the Top 5 most important actions (conversions) that you want a visitor to take when on your website?
2. Define 'lightly engaged' v 'heavily engaged' (visited 10 pages and spent 240+ seconds on your site). Keep an eye on these heavily engaged visitors!
3. How many clicks/pages it takes to complete the buying process and how long this process takes in seconds. This could be one set of criteria to define your segment. For example, if it takes 5 pages and 60 seconds on average, to buy a product, you could use this as engagement criteria.
4. Which sources of traffic drives 'engaged' visitors (and which key words engage more visitors)?

5. Which source of traffic results in a sale or a contract being signed?
6. What could happen after you have sold or converted - encourage visitors to buy more or to tell a friend or....?
7. How do we get people to stay on our site longer and activate them?
8. Is key content (pages or videos) being read/watched?
9. Do these pages have higher conversion rates?
10. What helps the nurturing process?

Who What Why – Summary

Behavioural Insights; the greatest untapped marketing asset

Most marketers are not exploiting the value of behavioural insights (capturing and consolidating customer behavioural data from multiple channels in a single database).

Despite newly automated processes (marketing automation), marketers are increasingly capturing this data, but not using it to build better marketing campaigns (Forrester, 2013).

The most sought after marketers today
are those that can manage
digital marketing and big data
(Rogers, 2013 at the Forbes Annual Conference)

Cookies, digital body language, big data and marketing automation collect a lot of useful customer data. It is possible, that with rigorous detailed analytics, specific rules, deep understanding of customers and careful planning, a marketer can give customers much more relevant content whilst automating many marketing activities to boost results. There's a brief explanation of How Cookies, Digital Body Language, Big Data and Marketing Automation Help You To Know Your Customer in the appendix 5.

All traffic is not equal
Those visitors that stay a few seconds, or move through the steps in your shopping cart, or enter your lead generation process, are more valuable to you than visitors who see your page for a few seconds and leave.' (Steve Jackson, Cult of Analytics).

'Stop wasting time on the stuff that doesn't help you.'

'Stop wasting time on the stuff that doesn't help you.'
Steve Jackson
Web analytics allows you to segment or filter visitors based on certain criteria but in a different way to the way marketers segment via demographic or psychographic data. You can set up a web analytics tool to view how visitors from a certain country, or city, act on your web site as compared to everyone else and see if there are differences. You can segment (filter) by (a) Marketing campaign to see what's converting best, (b) Unpaid traffic sources (referring websites), (c) Location; device; search phrase; site behaviour (engage); converters; visitor

---

> loyalty (segment by repeat visits, recency and frequency) and more. Steve Jackson (2011)

Create a business culture that 'craves customer knowledge'. Create an A/B culture (of split testing). Create a 'constant beta' culture. Your ability to ask great questions can determine the future of your business (and your career).

> **Will you be successful?**
> Asking great questions is one indicator of both your organisation's and your own, future success.

Think customers first - bring an empty chair
Amazon boss, Jeff Bezos, brings an empty chair to meetings to remind everyone of the omnipresence of the customer. Early on Bezos brought an empty chair into meetings so lieutenants would be forced to think about the crucial participant who wasn't in the room: the customer. Now that surrogate's role is played by specially trained employees, dubbed "Customer Experience Bar Raisers." When they frown, vice - presidents tremble. Rule no. 2 of Amazon boss, Jeff Bezos's 10 Leadership Lessons (Anders, 2012).

Ok, so that's the Customer Analysis section (Who, Why and How). It's easy now to see how "Our competitive advantage is understanding our customer, better than our competitors" (source unknown). Now let's explore competitors i.e. how you go about analysing your competitors.

1.2 Competitor Analysis

You have to know your competitors. Who are they? What are their strengths and weaknesses. How do they compete against you? How do you compete against them? Do you play to your strengths? Can you identify your competitive advantage (particularly from your customers' point of view).

Part of your competitor analysis explores your organisation's strengths and weaknesses (compared to your competitors). The external analysis on the other hand, includes opportunities and threats (both direct and indirect) in the external market place, such as trends and competitor strategies and tactics. You probably refer to this as a SWOT analysis.

So here are some questions you need to be able to answer about your competitors:
- How good are your competitors' websites?
- How good are your competitor's social media platforms?
- What social content works for your competitors?
- What Facbook content works for your competitors?
- What customers say about your competitors?
- What keywords work best in your competitors' ppc ads?
- What inbound links are your competitors using?
- Do you have enough share of voice?
- How big is your competitor's marketing team and budget?

- What are people saying about your competitors?
- Who are your new content marketing competitors?

Hyper Competition

Firstly, a warning: your business has moved into a new business environment - an environment packed with Hyper Competition. You have new, indirect competitors who you need to compete with using content marketing to gain visibility in the search results and social media. You are also in a borderless market with competitors from all over the world. You are also in a category-less market with competitors from other business sectors trying to acquire your customers.

Once upon a time, supermarkets sold groceries and petrol stations sold petrol. Today supermarkets sell petrol as well as pet insurance, BBQs and clothes, while petrol stations now also sell groceries, DVDs, fresh coffee, internet connection and more. We live in a category-less world determined by strength of brand and the ability to grow via share of wallet (selling a wider range to the same customer) rather than just share of market. Does the iWatch compete with Samsung, Swatch or Amazon?

Amazon and eBay mobile apps invite customers, while in another store, to scan in a product to see how much cheaper they can get it via the app (plus they deliver it to your door). So retailers have to have even better apps to compete inside your hypercompetitive pocket. Meanwhile Amazon can target ads at customers within a radius of one mile of a competing store.

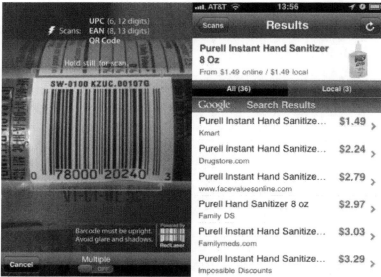

Price Comparison Apps are used in store for 'Showrooming'

Both Facbook and LinkedIn enable competitors to target their ads by age, interests, location or company. They can even target their ads at your employees (LinkedIn), your fans (Facbook) and even your website visitors (Google and other ad networks).

'If a retailer is not motivating people
to use its app in-store,
their customers may use a competitor's instead.'
(Gray, 2013)

You can monitor your competitor's website traffic, favourite pages, inbound links, key phrases, key phrases that work in organic search, phrases that work in online ads, and so much more. You can also find your competitors' customers and prospects attending a conference or an event (even a competitor's conference or event). You can even identify competitors' customers, e.g. if you are in the enterprise software business you can identify users of certain types of enterprise software from the enterprise software's tracking code used on their websites (see CrowdVu in the 'Who?' section).

Hyper competition hits the high street burger chains

We know you are going to go to Burger King because you tweeted "going to #BurgerKing". Competitors that are monitoring and data mining real-time conversations can offer you McDonald's coupons before you arrive at Burger King.

Are you more interesting than my wife?

That is the question many of your audience will ask, if they don't filter their personal emails from business emails. They have a combination of personal relationships and professional relationships coming into their in-tray. So you are not just competing with other suppliers, you are competing with everyone for my attention - from my wife or my best friend to my business colleagues. The crunch question first coined by Jay Bear (2013) is: 'Is your company more interesting to me than my wife?'

> **Illegal competition also competes**
> Some competition is legal and some is not so legal:
> Premier League to Clamp Down on Ilegal Streams
> after 30,000 Sites Taken Down Last Year – but it's
> still competition. 30,000 illegal competitors! Digital
> markets attract digital competition both legal and
> illegal.

How good are your competitors' websites?

There are many competitor monitoring services such
as Alexa.com which reveal information about most
sites' traffic, including: bounce rate; most popular
content; key phrases used; audience profile; daily
pages views; daily duration; where visitors come
from; inbound links. Paid subscriptions also get
demographics including location, age and gender.
Other services like Experian's Hitwise.com not only
reveal insights into competitor's search, affiliates,
display and social marketing strategies, they also:

- profile who visits your competitors' sites
- identify what is driving competitors' success
- benchmark the effectiveness of your existing
  customer acquisition strategies
- measure your website's performance against
  your competitors.

Compete.com also monitors competition and
benchmarks your performance against your industry

SimilarWeb allows you to compare website traffic stats, what your competitors are doing right and wrong, how to use this information to your advantage. The free version gives you all of the information below:

- Number of visitors (weekly in last 6 months)
- Duration (average)
- Page Views
- Bounce Rate
- Traffic Channel Sources include: direct, referrals (incl. breakdown) sites, search (incl. breakdown), social (incl. breakdown), mail and display
- Audience Geography, which geographic sources they come from
- Audience Interests: what other topics (incl. a topic word cloud), categories and websites these visitors also visited
- Website Ranking (global, within a country and by category)
- Keywords used to find the site (organic search and paid search)
- Similar Sites

The pro version includes: most popular pages, date range options, more details and more licensed seats (more of your team can use it).

'Find new customers by profiling who visits competitive sites.'
Steve Jackson, Cult of Analytics (2011)

How good are your competitors' social media platforms?

A social media audit identifies which platforms your competitors are using, how frequently, what kind of quality content, whether they have any following or communities following them, and more importantly, if their followers engage with them.

This is useful as it also identifies any potentially hot topics or issues with a competitor's products or services.

What social content works for your competitors?

Social Crawlytics is another free tool that reveals your competitor's most successful content and on which platforms it gets shared.

It also identifies the influencers who shared or referred to your competitor's content.

What Facbook content works for your competitors?

Research agencies can benchmark audience size, engagement, content that's popular and a lot more.

Here is, on the next page, a summary report from Simply Measured which shows number of fans (including new fans growth & share of audience), engagement levels for your own brand, the industry average and your bets competitor.

Best Buy Facebook Competitive Scorecard (January 2014)					
Your KPIs		Industry Benchmark		Industry Leader	
Best Buy Total	W/W Change	Industry Average	BB vs. Avg.	Macy's Total	BB vs. Leader
Audience					
Total Fans — 6,924,505	5.0%	5,219,036	133%	13,985,263	50%
New Fans — 10,840	12%	96,227	11%	181,021	6%
Fan Growth Rate — 0.2%	1%	1.9%	8%	1.3%	12%
Share of Audience — 13%	-1%	10%	133%	26%	50%
Engagement					
Total Engagement — 53,524	0%	168,874	32%	514,072	10%
Engagement Rate — 0.8%	5%	3.2%	24%	3.7%	21%
Engagement Per Post — 958	11%	3,748	26%	12,852	7%
Share of Engagement — 3.4%	4%	10.7%	32%	32.7%	10%
Content					
Brand Posts Per Day — 1.8	7%	1.7	109	1.3	140
User Posts Per Day — 62	1%	35	177%	26	241%
Responsiveness					
Response Rate — 85%	-2%	48%	177%	63%	135%
Responses Per Day — 53	5%	12	433%	16	326%

Source: How To Use Facbook Data To Analyze Your Competitors, Simply Measured 2014

What are people saying about your competitors?

Social listening tools let you hear what is being said about your brand and your competitors' brands and staff, as well as who is saying it. Social listening tools (many of which are free) allow you to drill down and engage in these conversations. This process of listening really helps you to develop your content strategy because you can listen to real needs being discussed and also what works for your competitors may well work for you also. Many social listening tools are discussed on my blog post, 'Social Listening Skills Part 1' which includes everything from free Google Alerts to other tools that monitor mentions (on the major social media platforms), to full blown sentiment analysis that collects all mentions of a brand and calculates a single score reflecting the positive or negative mood or sentiment.

Welcome to the world of infonomics.

Information has evolved from being a business by product to a business performance fuel, and now to an accepted form of legal tender. Organizations that cultivate, manage and are prepared to leverage this new-age currency, increasingly have an array of revenue streams and commercial options available to them. 'Welcome to the world of infonomics.'

(Laney, 2014)

Beware Of Bad Stats – Correlation Is Not Causation

'Have you ever noticed how we only win the World Cup under a Labour government?' British Prime Minister Harold Wilson, once said with tongue in cheek.

Or 37% of people who have a coffee mug with their company logo on it have been promoted within the last 6 months, compared to 8% of those people who did not have a coffee mug with their company logo on it. Yes it's OK to count these things, but I doubt that there's any statistical significance or association between owning a mug with a logo and getting promoted. Correlation is not causation.

What keywords work best in your competitors' ppc ads?

Eliminate Bad Keywords that waste your money. SpyFu finds your competitors' most successful ad copy which saves you spending time testing. It also helps you to 'weed out money-wasting keywords with negative match suggestions'. This also reveals your competitors' keyword strategies including every keyword they've bought on Adwords, every organic rank, and every ad variation in the last 6 years. Watch this 8 minute video 'Build Winning PPC Ad Copy Part 2, Spyfu Ad History' on Youtube.

What inbound links are your competitors using?

To see your competitors' inbound links, go to: Moz Open Site Explorer   www.opensiteexplorer.org and insert their name or their brand.

Do you have enough share of voice (sov)?

SOV can mean different things e.g. SOV PPC Ads, SOV PR/editorial, SOV SEO.
PPC people see SOV as a share of the total amount of impressions available to buy on a search or display platform whereas PR people see SOV as brand mentions out of all brand mentions in that sector. 'Mentions, segmented by vertical (social, news, blogs, etc.) often filtered by sophisticated Boolean queries that associate brand terms with keywords' (Weintraub, 2013). SOV SEO calculates how much traffic a brand can get for a particular key phrase as a percentage of all traffic generated for that same phrase.
See 'Control' section for more on SOV.

How big is your competitor's marketing team and budget?

A more manual approach involves a LinkedIn search on your competitor's name and any job titles that contain 'marketing', digital marketing' or 'communications'. The search produces an immediate list giving an initial indication of the size of the marketing department. Many researchers temporarily change their privacy restrictions to make their searches anonymous.

Many other companies only keep a small marketing team while subcontracting the marketing to external agencies. And others again do not conform to traditional job titles e.g. 'Director Of Mischief' (Paddy Power), or 'Chief Geek of Human Experiences' (Gilbert Geekery).

Remember Competition is only one click away.

Your Competitive Advantage

Knowing your own strengths and weaknesses is obviously important. So why do your customers buy from you rather than your competitor? Defining your competitive advantage (in the eyes of your customers) summarises almost everything we've covered up to now.

So why do your customers buy from you (instead of your competitors)?
Is there a specific, distinctive, reason?
Is it because you are:

- Technically Better
- Different product functions
- Looks Pleasing
- Tastier
- More Reliable
- Built To Last Longer
- More Easily Serviced
- Better Service Support
- More Flexible
- Faster Delivery
- More Mobile
- Readily Available
- Better Priced
- Better Brand
- Other?

Or

- You respond faster

- You respond to discussions online

- You have a presence online (across all main channels)

- You have a lot of added value online

- Or maybe you just happened to be in the right place at the right time?

- Other Reasons (emotional reasons)?

4 Crunch competitive questions
What is the best benefit of our product from customers' view?
How is our product/service completely unique?
Why would a customer buy from us and not competition?
When will the customer be better off buying from someone else?
List attributes and categorise as appealing to logic or emotion of customer.
How hard is it to understand the attribute?
(Steve Jackson, 2009)

Competitive Advantage 'The 3 Circle Model' by Urbany and Davis (2007)

Here's the very simple yet enlightening Urbany and Davis 3 circle model.

Consider the 3 core concepts of Company, Customers and Competition.

This is the Customer Circle (next page).
It represents the value sought by the customer – the requirements and benefits that they seek.

These requirements and benefits may include deeper values.

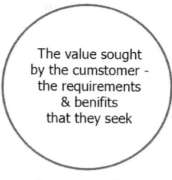

Customer Circle

Essentially the Customer Circle represents what the customer wants or what value the customer is seeking.

The second circle is your Company Circle. It represents the value customers perceive, or think, you offer to them

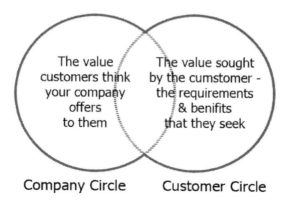

Company Circle   **Customer Circle**

Area 1, the overlapping area in the middle, is Positive Value. This is the value you are perceived to deliver to satisfy customer needs.

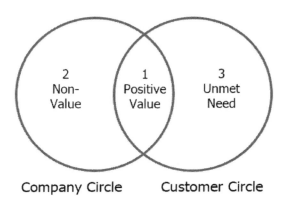

Company Circle   Customer Circle

Area 2 is 'Non-Value', which Urbany and Davis describe as the product or service you produce that the customer either doesn't care about, or perhaps, doesn't know about.

Area 3 is called 'Unmet Need'. Urbany and Davis describe these as customer needs that are not satisfied by your products and services and hence they offer a possible future growth opportunity.

The third circle (on the next page) is called the Competitor Circle.

This is the final piece of the jig saw.

It soon opens up a whole new way of thinking......

The competitor circle represents what value does the customer perceive in your competitor's offering.

You can see it's a Venn diagram.

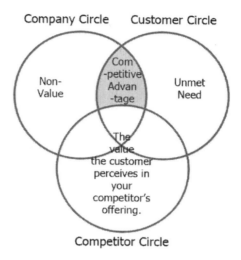

Competitor Circle

The overlapping shaded area at the top is 'the pure definition of competitive advantage'. As urbany and davis say, this is the value that you create that matters to customers, but, that is different to competition. **This is why people choose us.**'

So the next big question for you is 'What's your competitive advantage?'

This excellent question forces you to begin the process of defining your distinctive competitive advantage. If you ask six different members of your team, you might get six different answers.

You can watch Professor Joe Urbany present his approach to Competitive Strategy in 3 Minutes on video 'Competitive Strategy In 3 Minutes' by 25Urbany. This is highly recommended viewing.

Hidden competitors lurk

They never saw it coming. Spirit level manufacturers never imagined that they might one day compete with phones or free spirit level apps. Now this category-less, indirect, competitor is eating into their business. So relentless improvement is required as new (direct and indirect competitors) continually emerge. See how wonderfully disruptive 'digital sizzle' can be in the Objectives section.

1.3 Partners and Intermediaries

Your Situation Analysis should also include an analysis of your partners to see which works best whether they are intermediaries (e.g. retailers) or other strategic alliances (marketing marriages) giving you new routes to market. 'Partners' are the 8th P when talking about the marketing mix. Partners require resources e.g. clear communications to manage, measure and nurture partner relationships, hence some organisations recognise this and have partner managers and partnership directors.

- **Intermediaries** – such as price comparison sites or aggregators
- **Affiliates** – your network of sites that promote your product
- **Influencers** – your network of bloggers, journos, tweeters
- **Marketing Marriages/Strategic Alliances** – whose brands add value to each other's customers and target audiences overlap – sharing databases or campaign costs.
- **Link partners** – partners who help to boost your SEO
- **Syndication partners** – partners who will share content online
- **Advertising partners** – whose sites share ad space in the long-term

Is it worth maintaining all of these partners? Or should you reallocate your resources? Your Partnership Analysis will tell you.

Copetitors

Today, it is not uncommon for some of your partners (or even customers) to compete with you on some of their portfolio of products/services. We call these 'copetitors'. Perhaps some of your competitors may partner with you on some of your other products/services?

So your partnership analysis should identify what works and what doesn't, or at least what is restricting success, so that it can be fixed.

1.4 Competencies Analysis

Your Performance or Results Analysis will already indicate some of your strengths and weaknesses. However, it's good to know these before you start spending your budget and the results start coming in.

Here's a nice quick Digital Marketing Capability Analysis which you can take any time you are ready to face the reality of where you, or your organisation is, in terms of digital competencies.

It explores your Digital Marketing Competencies in 7 aspects using a score from 1-5 (5 being 'Optimised').

- Your Strategic approach
- Evaluation and performance improvement process
- Management buy-in to investment in digital marketing
- Resourcing and structure for digital including integration
- Data and infrastructure or platforms
- Integrated customer communications across Paid-Owned-Earned media
- Integrated customer experiences across desktop and mobile devices

This is Smart Insights' capability assessment. It helps you to know where your organisation is from Stage 1 'Initial' (with no strategy, no KPIs etc.) to Stage 2 'Managed' (with prioritised activities and some KPIs etc.) to Stage 3 'Defined' (with clearly defined vision & strategy, Quality bases KPIs, partial integration of data and systems etc.) to Stage 4 'Quantified' (KPIs with weighted attribution, integrated systems etc.) to Stage 5 'Optimised' (Lifetime Value KPIs, integral part of strategy etc.).

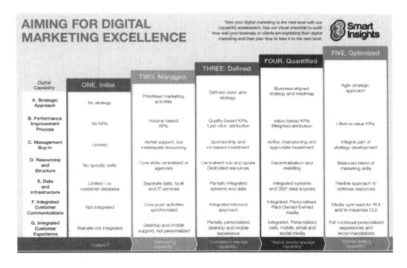

Apologies as this is very small print – is too small to read. You will find it in www.SmartInsights.com called 'Digital Marketing Capability Analysis'.

Obviously an 'Optimised' organisation has a competitive advantage over an organisation that is only at the 'Initial' stage of its digital marketing maturity. The strategy choice which then emerges is whether to build a newly structured marketing department or employ external agencies.

The Strategy section will mention this again and you can see a newly structured marketing department in the Action section.

1.5 Performance/Results Analysis

The results of all your efforts are summarised by the Key Performance Indicators (KPIs). They never lie.

Never look at numbers in isolation (particularly when looking at results). We need to see them in the context of previous periods (to see if there is a trend) and also we need to see them compared to competition to see how we have performed comparatively.

For example, £10m sales is great news if we only made £5m last year. But if we made £20m last year then it's terrible news.

But what if the market had shrunk from £100m to £20m? Our market share would have increased from 10% (£10m/£100m) to 25% (£5/£20m).

The next strategic question is do we want to stay in a market this size?

We'll look at strategy later.

Meanwhile here's a selection of typical KPIs which can be used to analyse performance.

Objectives

KPI	Results Previous Period	Objective Current Period	Results Current Period filled in later (in the Control section)
ROI (Return On Investment)			
Sales - units - value			
Market Share - units - value			
Market Leader Number (in top 5)			
Awareness Level (offline survey)			
Preference Level (offline survey)			
NPS Score (Net Promoter Score)			
Sentiment Score (incl. competitor comparison)			
Website/Blog Unique Visitors Average Duration Subscribers to updates/Newsletter Leads generated			

Objectives (contd.)

KPI	Results Previous Period	Objective Current Period	Results Current Period filled in later
Cost Per Visitor (website)			
Cost Per Like (Facbook)			
Cost Per Lead			
Cost Per Customer Acquisition			
Cost Per Customer Retention			
Database Size			
Prospects/Leads			
Customers			
Advocates			
Influencers			

Specific Web Site KPIs

KPI	Results Previous Period	Object-ive Current Period	Results Current Period filled in later
Site Visits			
Unique Visitors			
Bounce Rate			
Duration			

Specific Web Site KPIs (contd.)

KPI	Results Previous Period	Objective Current Period	Results Current Period filled in later
Page Views passive engagement			
Most Popular Page(s)/downloads			
Engagement - Downloads			
Engagement - Likes/Favourites			
Engagement - Comments			
Engagement - Shares			
Engagement - Registrations/Newsletter			
Churn Rate			
Conversions - Leads & Sales			
Sales (all sales)			
Task Completion			
SCAR (Shopping Cart Abandonment Rate)			
Satisfaction Score			
NPS Score			
Sentiment Score			
Share of Voice			
Social Media Platforms – repeat for each platform			
Followers/Likes – engagement etc.			

There are many different approaches, to KPI desktops, layouts...

The next approach turns the pyramid upside down and into the sales funnel, starting with number of visitors, % engagement and sales.

The basic sales funnel

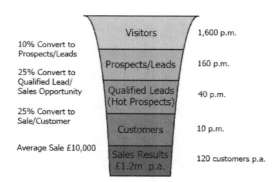

An organisation's performance can also be summarised by its Sales Funnel

You will see how the sales funnel and all of the KPIs can be used to set crystal clear objectives, in chapter 2, Objectives.

1.6 Market Trends – opportunities and threats

In the Customer Analysis section I mentioned some trends in the way customers digest information – shorter attention spans, more visual, multi-tasking, mobile etc.
In addition, every market has its own specific trends that affect the market. Marketers must be aware of them, never ignore them and always adjust their plans accordingly.

The **PEST factors** (political, economic, social and technological) or PESTED (add environment and demographics), need to be monitored to identify trends that can affect your business either as an opportunity or a threat. Take politics briefly; laws and regulations can affect your business. Here are two examples:

Deregulation affects many markets
TTIP is the Transatlantic Trade Investment Partnership between the USA and the EU, criticised by some as allowing US corporations to sue EU governments for loss of profits caused by a government's laws or regulations. Anti TTIP videos on Youtube suggest that American tobacco companies are already suing the Australian

government for loss of profits since banning persuasive cigarette packaging.

Do some markets need more regulation than others?

Increasing law suits threaten all marketers

Many industry sectors regulate themselves. In fact advertising has its own code of practice to which marketers must adhere. In addition, there are laws that mostly protect the customer from being exploited by unfair or false advertising.

Red Bull energy drink offered to refund $10 (with a maximum cap of $13m) to anyone who consumed their product after 2002 since their 'Red Bull Gives You Wings' campaign was sued as false advertising. There is a debate about the caffeine levels being less than a cup of coffee. So Red Bull settled out of court to avoid the distraction. Most marketers may now look even more carefully at the promises they make via their advertising.

Now let's look at a few digital trends that suddenly combine to make customer analysis and subsequent communications an awful lot deeper, easier and more exciting for us marketers:

- Customer Data is everywhere
- Data Storage Costs keep falling
- Big Data is also everywhere
- The Internet Of Things is here
- Cloud Wars
- Content Wars
- Shrinking Customer Attention Spans

Customer data is everywhere

We leave digital trails everywhere when we browse, click, scan or fill in a form. This data can be cross referenced with social media platforms to gather extra data. Additional third party databases can be used to layer on more information.
Search, social, and analytics can be combined with some clever APIs (Application Programming Interfaces) which help software components to interact with each other. This means that there is a golden opportunity to drill down into a gold mine of customer data from many different sources (both online and offline).

Data storage costs keep falling

As the cost of data storage comes tumbling down and data integration/analysis tools get cleverer, potentially large volumes of useful customer data is emerging almost everywhere.

Big Data is also everywhere

Refers to relatively large amounts of structured and unstructured data that require machine-based systems and technologies in order to be fully ☐nalysed. 'The much-hyped term has inspired a slew of definitions, many of which involve the concepts of massive volume, velocity and variety of information. In other words, what turns data into Big Data is the amount of information, and the speed at which it can be created, collected and analysed.' (Kaye 2013).

Big Data is everywhere
Here are 10 Useful Ways Big Data Is Used – That You Probably Didn't Know
– from Lady Gaga To Premature Babies

The Internet of Things

After the fixed internet of the 1990s, came the mobile internet of the 2000s connecting 2-6 billion. Then came the IoT connecting 28 billion things from smartphones, to watches, glasses, cars, clothes, your home, and your business.
The Harvard Business Review Global Editions suggests The Sectors Where the Internet of Things Really Matters (Jankowski, 2014)

Cloud wars

The marketing cloud is the marketing nirvana – a place, or a hub, where marketers automate and integrate all customer data, automatically analyse it then continuously and automatically serve highly relevant engaging content across multi- channels at just the right time on the right platform to the right customer. Fast moving marketers will use the marketing cloud (multichannel marketing automation, content management tools, social media tools and analytics platforms – more later) to create a wall around their customers, which competitors will consequently find difficult to break down (particularly because of customers' changing behaviours). This is now a race towards an automated integrated digital marketing hub.

CMOs will outspend CIOs on IT
With this kind of new opportunity (integrated digital hub) it's not surprising to see Gartner predict that CMOs will outspend CIOs on IT in 2017 (McLellan, 2012) as the 'Race Towards the Automated Integrated Digital Marketing Hub Is On' (Akhtar 2014).

Content Wars
Meanwhile Content Wars are drowning some customers in a rising sea of marketing content yet many marketers don't know why some content works and some doesn't which creates a situation that 'leads to more content being created.' (Belicove, 2013)

A sea of content
Every two days we create as much information as we did in the last two thousand years. Eric Schmidt, CEO Google effectively said this back in 2010 (Kirpatrick2010)

Shrinking customer attention spans

As customers' attention spans shrink, email open rates plummet and social media engagement nosedives, the information fatigued, multi-tasked, semi-burnt out customer has limited time and desire to give their personal data to 'other' companies. So first in wins (first to get the sign ups wins). The 'connected customer' expects the 'Internet of Everything' (everything connected) to deliver highly relevant, added value content and experiences constantly.

So change appears to be accelerating – whether shrinking attention spans (social changes), quantum data shifts (technology), new regulations & laws (political) or fundamental economic cycles (economics) that grow or shrink your market, the PEST factors need constant monitoring.

Summary: Situation analysis

So once you thoroughly know your situation

- Customers (who, why and how)
- Competitors (direct and indirect)
- Competencies (strengths and weaknesses)
- Market trends (opportunities and threats)
- Performance/Results (what worked and what didn't work)

You will then see what your Distinctive Competitive Advantage (DCA) is. You can then decide if this fits with what customers want and with future market trends. You can make strategic choices about whether to nurture your current DCA or develop another DCA later in the Strategy section.

Meanwhile, you must create a culture of 'customer obsession'. You and your team must master these three big questions 'Who, Why and How'. Listen to your customers online (as well as offline). Get the technical infrastructure to support dynamic, cross-channel conversations with customers and the subsequent analytics to help you to find more of the same type of customers (once you know who you are after) and to help you to make better informed decisions (see Tactics section).

Finally, remember Sun Tzu's words at the start of this section:

Those who triumph,
Compute at their headquarters
a great number of factors
prior to a challenge.

Those who are defeated,
compute at their headquarters
a small number of factors
prior to a challenge.

Much computation brings triumph.
Little computation brings defeat.
How much more so with no computation at all.

By observing only this,
I can see triumph or defeat.

With your Situation Analysis completed you know where you really are in the market place. Now let's clarify where you want to go – with some realistic objectives.

Chapter 2

Objectives

Although some argue that the most important goals or objectives are simply to increase:

- Revenue
- Margin
- Customer Satisfaction
- Brand Value (controlling the brand promise increases the brand value)

I take a slightly different view and start with the ultimate objectives which are the Mission and Vision statements, followed by the typical KPIs which include the above in more detail.

2.1 Mission

This is your raison d'etre (the reason your organisation exists). This must include how you make the world a better place – how you ultimately help customers and stakeholders. It should also demonstrate some CSR (Corporate Social Responsibility) while giving direction for the organisation. Google's mission statement is a good mission statement: 'to organize the world's information and make it universally accessible and useful'.

2.2 Vision

A vision statement is more organisation orientated (as opposed to a mission statement which is more market orientated or customer/community orientated). A vision states where the organisation sees itself in 3, 5 or 10 years' time. Imagine writing a headline in the New York Times or the FT for your business: 'XYZ is the number one company in the world (or Asia, China or Beijing, etc). So the vision sets major goals for how successful your organisation will be in the future. This includes size of turnover, size of organisation, size of market share, local, national or global, position in the market place (number 1, 2 or 3).

After this comes the typical KPIs. Here is the KPI Pyramid (adopted from Joe Pulizzi, 2013).

2.3 KPIs

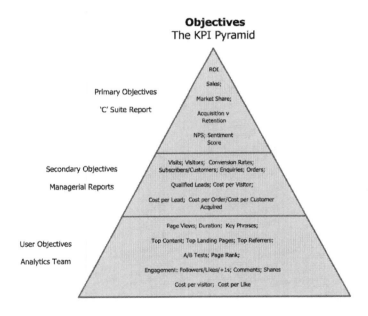

Objectives
The KPI Pyramid

Key Performance indicators can be broken down in more detail right down to revenue contribution per channel (or tool), Cost per visit/enquiry/lead/like and sale broken down by channel. Note: awareness levels, preference levels and market position are often measured via offline surveys.

You can also turn the KPI Pyramid upside down (and select fewer KPI criteria) to get the sales funnel approach to objectives. The next approach turns the pyramid upside down and into the 'sales funnel', starting with number of visitors, % engagement and eventually sales objectives.

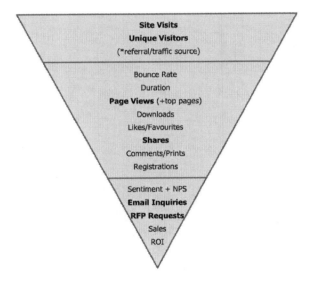

The Objectives Pyramid turned upside down becomes a sales funnel highlighting a selection of KPIs

Certain click behaviour indicates whether a visitor is a prospect. It could be determined by the amount of time ('duration') they spent on specific product pages and perhaps whether they checked the price pages. A prospect can be categorised as a qualified lead if,say, they came back a second time plus watched the product demonstration video plus read some customer reviews and checked the pricing page again. So goals or objectives can be set for number of visitors, leads, qualified leads, customers and total sales revenue by using the classic sales funnel approach.

The Sales Funnel

10% Convert to Prospects/Leads

25% Convert to Qualified Lead/ Sales Opportunity

25% Convert to Sale/Customer

Average Sale £10,000

Visitors

Prospects/Leads

Qualified Leads (Hot Prospects)

Customers

Sales Objective £1.2m p.a.

The Sales Funnel can also be used to set objectives

If you know your conversion rates, it is easy to set objectives in terms of the number of visitors you need to generate a specific number of customers. If, for example, the sales objective is £1.2m (and the average sale is £10,000), then the organisation needs 1,600 visitors each month with 10% of these becoming prospects (160 pcm) . If 25% of these prospects become qualified leads (i.e. 40 qualified leads per month p.m.). If 25% of these qualified leads, on average, convert to becoming customers, they will get 10 new customers pcm which is 120 new customers p.a.

KPIs
You can, and should, go much deeper with your objectives. By having detailed objectives for many different KPIs (Key Performance Indicators), you have more control over your organisation's performance. Here are some KPIs again (see next page).

Objectives
KPIs (some typical KPIs used online)

You can review the different types of objectives in the Situation Analysis chapter (and also in the Control chapter). For now, here is a summary list of popular KPI Objectives used online.

KPIs **Objectives** (some typical KPIs used online)

KPI	Period 1	Period 2	Period 3
Site Visits			
Unique Visitors			
Bounce Rate			
Duration			
Page Views passive engagement			
Most Popular Page/s			
Most popular downloads			
Engagement - Downloads			
Engagement - Likes/Favourites			
Engagement - Comments			
Engagement - Shares			
Engagement - Registrations/Newsletter			
Churn Rate (% of followers you lose)			

Conversions - Leads & Sales			
Sales (all sales)			
Market Share			
ROI			
Task Completion			
Satisfaction Score			
NPS Score			
Sentiment Score			
Share of Voice			

Social Media Platforms – repeat for each one			
Followers/Like – engagement etc.			

2.4 The Race Approach to Objectives

The Smart Insights RACE framework (Reach, Act, Convert and Engage)
is another way of looking at objectives as the customer moves through the customer life cycle from initial contact to lifetime loyalty. Each stage can be quantified as an objective.

Reach is about increasing awareness of a brand and encouraging visits to a website or social media presence, e.g. to increase new visits to your site per month by 5% or 5,000.

Act means encouraging initial interaction with content which then generate leads, e.g. to increase leads by 1% or 1,000 per month.

Convert is the ultimate conversion to sales achieved online or offline, e.g. increase online sales conversion rate by 10% from 2% to 2.2%.

Engage means post-sales engagement designed to create long term loyalty and advocacy, e.g. to generate x% engagement from existing customers or to generate x number of 5 star reviews, shares or likes.

You can see more examples of KPIs in the Control section and, in particular, where VQVC goals go beyond site visitor volume and include measures of site visit Quality, Value and Cost. This is a good example of Control/Metrics measuring performance, to inform Situation

Analysis and help to refine the next set of KPI targets.

More on RACE on SmartInsights.com

2.5 The 5Ss Approach To Objectives

One other, very different approach which I developed in the '90s when the internet first emerged, was 'The 5Ss': Sell, Serve, Save, Speak and Sizzle.

- Sell means 'sales' targets, both online (if relevant) and offline sales influenced by online.
- Serve sets customer service targets but also inspires better service (see Sizzle).
- Save means to save both money and time (for both the customer and the organisation) by delivering an efficient service.
- Speak means conversations, listening carefully and participating. Engagement is another measure of 'speak'.
- Sizzle is the digital sizzle or magic that delivers added value or digital sizzle to a brand which you simply cannot get offline.

2.6 Inspirational Objectives

All objectives, other than Sizzle, should have numbers (timescales and metrics or goals and compared to a benchmark/average). Sizzle can have numbers and certainly should be inspirational, e.g. Sir David Ramsbotham, Chief Inspector of Her Majesty's Prisons, changed the key objective from 'number of escapees' to 'number of repeat offenders'.

National Semiconductor's Sizzle objective was so visionary that it created sustainable competitive advantage. 'Develop a website that wows our customers so much they'll never leave us' was the enlightened CEO's brief. See the full story in the appendices.

The Sistine Chapel in Rome Digital now has global digital sizzle so good that the website's customer experience actually beats the real life customer experience when physically visiting the chapel.

The Sistine Chapel is a good example of digital sizzle. Arguably, the best website in the world with only two buttons/tabs. Yet it delivers a wonderful experience for those that want to soak it in and see it up close and uninterrupted. In fact, you can climb the walls and, if you want, stand under the great ceiling to enjoy the unique view that Michelangelo had as he stood on his giant scaffolding while painting the stunning ceiling way back in 1512. This is digital sizzle.

Visit the Vatican.VA Sistine Chapel to see Michelangelo's stunning frescos. You can move around, walk up the walls, zoom in on the ceilings and see the detail – something you simply cannot do when you visit the chapel. Don't forget to turn on your audio also.

Digital Sizzle adds value
It's interesting to see how making Sizzle an objective can sometimes shake things up. 'Let's add digital Sizzle to create added value' or to 'wow' our customers or to give them a stunning customer experience. Incidentally, this can also create competitive advantage. Here are a few summary examples:

- Sistine chapel digital experience widens the reach (and interaction/experience) of visiting the Sistine chapel. Indeed many visitors say the online experience is better than the 'real thing'.

- Nike + iPod digital technology can change a solo run into a competitive global community run with other runners across the world. Effectively, changing the customer experience from a running shoe into competing in a live global running club.

- National Semiconductor, as mentioned earlier, embraced digital and created so much added digital value to their website that their customers simply cannot work without it (see appendix for more).

Technology will be at the centre of every product and service
We will soon have 'the super-efficient chips that can be empowered by ambient energy combined with cloud technology will soon put digital technology at the centre of every product and service.'
(Satell, 2012)

More and more services are converging and moving from the physical into the digital world. In fact, it is here that all products become services as added digital value services are layered onto the fundamental product.

Marketing objectives and marcomms objectives
One final point; some organisations separate marketing objectives and marcomms objectives. Marketing objectives are action orientated, e.g. sales, clicks and conversions, while marcomms objectives are mentally orientated e.g. awareness, preference, positioning, and attitudes which are measured by surveys (offline or online).

Objectives Summary
From Mission, to Vision, to KPIs, to the 5Ss, crystal clear objectives help the organisation to focus on what needs to be done. Objectives also give

direction. Objectives, including 'Sizzle', can also motivate teams.

Sensible and quantifiable objectives are easy to set once you have done a thorough Situation Analysis as you can see how you performed against the previous period's objectives. The analysis reveals strengths, weaknesses and market trends which will guide you towards making better objectives.

These objectives will be measured (some on a daily basis and others on a quarterly basis). The Control section measures performance against the objectives set.

The Control section also specifies what gets measured and by whom, when, and most importantly, what happens with this information – what kind of marketing decisions will be made as a result of measuring metrics.

Objectives are measured in the Control section,
which in turn, feeds the next period's Situation Analysis

Chapter 3

Strategy

SOSTAC® is a registered trade mark of www.PRSmith.org

> "All men can see the tactics whereby I conquer,
> what none can see is the strategy
> out of which victory is evolved."
> Sun Tzu, The Art of War

Strategy answers 'How do we get there?'

Situation Analysis answers 'where are we now?'
Objectives clarify 'where do we want to go?' and
Strategy summarises 'how do we get there?'
Strategy requires the ability to see the big picture.
Yet strategy is in fact the smallest, yet arguably the
most difficult, part of a plan. There are nine key
strategic components which you need to consider
carefully. We'll explore these in a few minutes.

Strategy harnesses capabilities

Strategy requires coherent thinking that harnesses
capabilities (existing or those that can be acquired) to
tackle problems and exploit opportunities. It is difficult
to find examples of great digital marketing strategies.
Perhaps because digital is not isolated as a digital
strategy, but rather it should be part of a broader
marketing strategy.

Strategy is the big picture

Blue Ocean Strategy avoids the 'strategic hell' of
undifferentiated products competing in price wars
until someone gets squeezed out. A Blue Ocean
Strategy makes competition irrelevant and creates an
uncontested market space. Apple iPhones and iPods
did this. See more in appendix 6. Porter's Strategic
Competitive Advantage gives companies 3 strategic
options of competing by: (1) product differentiation

(includes positioning), (2) targeting niche target markets (includes targeting) or (3) competing by low cost (includes targeting and positioning). The Ansoff Matrix looks at target markets and products and generates four strategic options for growth: (1) sell more existing product into existing markets or (2) new markets or (3) sell new product into existing markets or (4) sell new products into new markets (double axes of risk!)

These are all marketing strategies that involve product decisions, in fact all of the marketing mix. We are going to specifically look at digital marketing strategies and use a relatively easy 9 Key Components checklist to build your digital marketing strategy. But first, let's start with a tragic marketing story – where the wrong marketing strategy killed a great product – the world's first e-Car.

3.1 Strategy – The Difference: Success and Failure

Lousy Marketing Strategy Kills A Great Product

This is an offline example that demonstrates two critical components that apply to every digital marketing strategy. I'm still frustrated and angry about why this excellent innovation failed. Why? Because of a lousy marketing strategy. I hope you will see the major strategic errors before I highlight them. So here we go, once upon a time, a clever British technology inventor, Sir Clive Sinclair, created a radical innovation, the world's first electric car (or e-Car). He called it the Sinclair C5.

The Sinclair C5

Launched in 1980s, the C5 targeted 3 groups: Women going shopping; men commuting to the station and kids playing sport during the summer. Distributed via electricity board retail stores across all UK high streets and retailing at £399. It needed to be charged every 70 miles and had a max speed of 30 mph. It was tested in large warehouses with simulated road experiences.

A nightmare unfolding
At the time I was a young marketing lecturer working in the heart of the City of London.

I wrote to Sir Clive Sinclair at Sinclair Vehicles to tell them they were making a terrible marketing strategy mistake which would destroy the innovative e-Car but which we could fix without any fee required. They wrote back to me and promised to get the marketing manager to call me. He never did, despite two calls from me.

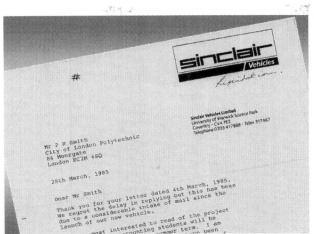

Trying to save the world's first electric car from self destruction

The company soon went bust. The sad thing is that it could have and should have been a success. It did not require any more product development funds nor any product redesign. There was a market for this product. So what do you think was wrong with the marketing strategy and what marketing strategy could have saved it? Stop for a moment and think.

Firstly, positioning the C5 as a car killed it dead. Across every purchase criteria for a car (speed, safety, in-car entertainment, size etc.) it scored lowest. Secondly, targeting shoppers, commuters and kids was never going to work. There were so many other segments which could have been targeted including the greens, hot climate countries with holiday makers, or B2B markets such as airports and exhibition conference centres.

The remaining stock was liquidated and sold to a smart marketer who repositioned the C5 electric car as a 'Space Rider' fun novelty item targeted at young holiday fun lovers in Spain. He then addressed the marketing mix: doubled the price, distributed via moped rental shops in Spanish holiday resorts and with very simple limited promotion he sold the factory stock (at twice the purchase price) within a short period. This is what he did.

Targeting and positioning – two classic components of strategy

You can see businesses and teams of people working harder and harder, longer and longer hours, yet still failing to achieve their KPI objectives. If you get the strategy wrong, the tactics will be wrong and no matter how hard you work it will just get more and more difficult to achieve your KPI Objectives.

'There's no point rowing harder, if you are rowing in the wrong direction.'
World guru, author and former head of McKinsey, Tokyo, Kenichi Ohmae

---

It is critical that you get these two major strategic components correct:

- Target Markets means breaking markets into segments and carefully selecting the right segments to target, i.e. targeting the 'low hanging fruit'. These are the customers that you can easily reach and who really want your product or service.

- Positioning means how you want to be perceived or positioned in the minds of your target market(s); ideally where there is a real customer need and little competition.

Two more recent repositioning examples are e-cigarettes and Intel. Although subtle changes, these are big decisions.

e-cigarette company, blu-e-cig, want to reposition their product from:
- 'an alternative method to give up smoking' to
- 'a lifestyle choice for smokers'

Jacob Fuller, CEO Blu-e-cig says 'Our biggest mistake was to call it an e-cigarette - an alternative method to give up smoking." (Benady, 2014)

Intel recently made a bold strategic decision by changing their positioning from:
- 'High quality technology products' to
- 'Leader in technology breakthroughs'.

Intel's strategy is to position itself as a leader in technology breakthroughs targeting generation Y (born in the 1960s and '70s) by associating Intel with innovation in music, art and lifestyle, using social media to leverage offline real events.

This is a major strategic decision that will drive all of their tactics including: developing an online community forum called IT Galaxy; a B2B game IT Manager III: Unseen Forces; outdoor 3D projections; partnering with edgy magazine 'Vice' to launch The Creators Project and Facbook app The Museum Of Me; Appointed Will.i.am, Black Eyed Peas, as director of creative innovation as well as the more traditional print display, Google search, TV ads, social media, PR and training programmes (for store assistants and re-sellers).

So strategy drives tactics (not the other way around). Let's look at all 9 Key components for your digital marketing strategy. We've already mentioned two of them – positioning and targeting.

Watch the 'Museum Of Me' video on Youtube

Just before we move onto the 9 components of a digital marketing strategy, it is worth emphasising that positioning directly influences your Online Value Proposition. Your OVP answers your online visitor's question 'What's in it for me?' Do your website, your content and your social media platforms all express a clear OVP?

3.2 Positioning and Your Online Value Proposition

A company website offers great opportunities to offer added value to the customer experience which simply isn't available offline. This added value can vary from new types of content to entertain or content to inform people how to use your products, to new types of interactive services like a customer community or some 'sizzle' like the Sistine Chapel digital experience mentioned in the Objectives section. Many businesses miss out on the digital opportunity to add new types of value from digital channels.

Online value proposition

An online value proposition is closely tied to your brand's positioning which answers questions such as: Who are we? What do we offer? Which markets do we serve? What makes us different? And the customer's crunch question: What's in it for me? which needs to be answered within seconds of landing on a website.

OVP is more than just selling

But the OVP is more than just a selling proposition since it shows what you can offer by way of content, products, services and experiences to engage online customers. The OVP extends this difference in that it identifies the reasons why customers will click on, return to, register or buy from your site and ideally, feel motivated enough to share their experience – the last point being key in an age where the customer increasingly defines the brand.

OVP communicates customer benefits

The customer value proposition should succinctly state the intrinsic benefits a visitor will get from staying on a particular website, viewing some content, web service or functionality and how that ties to your overall product or service. It cannot simply be your brand promise or a more general customer value proposition stuck online, since that misses the point that someone is on your site now and asking themselves 'what's in this for me?' Content marketing can be at the heart of developing many OVPs.

OVP – part of ongoing integrated communications

Your OVP should be developed around your audience personas, support commercial goals and be communicated as part of ongoing integrated communications to encourage prospects to experience this value. The OVP can only be developed after the positioning has been decided.

Targeting and Positioning are just two of the 9 key components of digital marketing strategy. Let's explore all 9 now.

3.3 Components of Digital Marketing Strategy

TOPPP SITE (9 Key Components)

Here are 9 key components to consider when building your digital marketing strategy. You do not have to use all 9 key components in your digital marketing strategy. In fact, the strategy excerpts I'll show you later only include a selection of these 9 key components. You may find some components overlap/integrate. This is good. Your strategy doesn't have to be in the same order as TOPPP SITE. Feel free to move the components around to suit your strategy. Now let's consider each of the 9 components to help you to build a crystal clear digital marketing strategy.

Target Markets (essential)
Objectives (it's helpful to summarise what objectives the strategy should deliver)
Positioning (essential)
Processes (strategy can involve new processes - these may overlap with integration)
Partnership (strategic alliances and marketing marriages can make marketing easy)

Sequence (or stages, e.g. Develop Credibility before Raising Visibility)
Integration (of data – this may overlap with 'Processes' – major opportunity here)
Tactical Tools (or channels: list the priority tools PPC, SEO, email or PR and Content)
Engagement (what level of the Ladder Of Engagement is required?)

Let's take a look at each of these briefly.

Target markets
Target markets need to be defined very clearly. Today we have many new variables (or filters) to help marketers identify targets. Time and effort spent carefully analysing and discussing who is/are the most ideal target market/s is time well spent.

Positioning
Positioning is so strategic that you really don't want to be changing this each year. Positioning means precisely how you want to be positioned (or perceived) in the minds of your target customers. Note: Positioning is the foundation for brand propositions (what's in it for the customer) and ultimately, the customer experience (CX). In fact, defining the brand, the OVP and the CX are part of strategy. OVP and CX also influence the marketing mix (tactical decisions), e.g. exclusive products online; differential pricing; exclusive online promotions; prioritising which channels; online distribution partners etc. These details are addressed in your Tactics section.

The Classic Repositioning:
from Sick Child to Healthy Adult

Lucozade repositioned itself from a 'sick child's drink' to a 'healthy adult's drink'. They followed the market trends: the demographic shift from a massive child market (baby boom) in the 60s to a bulging 40 year old market in the noughties (2000s). They also followed the trend towards 'healthy living'. This repositioning strategy drives changes across all of

---

the marketing mix tactics from chemist shop distribution and 'mother and child' ads to sports celebrity ads and CocaCola style distribution into shops, restaurants and offices.

Objectives
It is always worth double checking that your strategy actually delivers the 'big' objectives (Mission and Vision) as well as the typical sales, market share and ROI KPIs. Strategy without some reference to objectives is, not surprisingly, unlikely to achieve those objectives. Hence some organisations like to see the main objectives referred to when presenting their strategies. Deciding which is a priority objective - Customer Acquisition or Customer Retention - is a strategic decision (see more later).

Process
If you are introducing a new approach, a new process, a system or even new way of thinking, this can be strategic, e.g introducing marketing automation or insisting analytics are used to measure, understand and drive all future decisions; nurturing a 'Constant Beta Culture' or introducing a new customer service process integrating telephone, Twitter and Facbook. See the Action section for the detailed process of producing great marketing content.

Finally do you need a new marketing team structureor employ external agencies to manage the process of marketing? See what a new marketing department looks like in the appendices.

Partnerships

Partnership – introducing or strengthening or reducing strategic partnership/marketing marriages/marketing alliances. Are there potential partners out there whose customers would welcome your organisation's products or services? Selecting the right partner can firstly give you access to a much bigger target market and secondly, strengthen your brand. But remember partnerships have to benefit both parties, with clear goals, roles and responsibilities – 'the devil is in the detail'.

Sequence or stages

Develop credibility before raising visibility. How many businesses get that one wrong? How many major TV ad campaigns or content marketing and social media platforms drive traffic to websites that don't work? In addition there may be other steps such as building awareness, then brand preference before seeking sales, or other stages in a campaign such as acquiring endorsers; establishing relationships and advocates, followed by campaign rollout. Another approach to some of the stages you want to move customers through is Dave Chaffey's RACE (Reach means increasing awareness and encouraging visits; Act means initial interaction; Convert means conversion to sales; Engage means post-sales engagement designed to create long term loyalty and advocacy). Customer acquisition v customer retention decisions wil be determined by the objectives you have set earlier.

Integration

Integrating customer data online and offline is a strategic decision. From click behaviour data (digital body language), to registration data, to social media data to CRM (Customer Relationship Management) to purchase behaviour, to post-purchase contact data. Layering it with external data from third party databases. 'Having social data as well as a complete history of your leads' and customers' activity in one place is invaluable to your company, because it means you can finally stop wasting time on what doesn't work, as well as equipping your sales team with the information to help them close more deals.' (Toner, 2014)

Process and integration
Integrate Social Data With Your CRM or Contacts Database. Introduce an integrated customer profiling process into both outbound and inbound campaigns.

Tactical tools

Tactics (or channels) will be explored in more detail in the Tactics section. Your marketing strategy should, however, identify which are the major tactical tools (or channels) you will be using. Your brand, the customer experience you wish to deliver, the nature of your audience and the strategy you wish to adopt will define which tactical tools to use in your campaigns. Should you prioritise with a major PPC ad campaign, email campaigns, nurture an affiliate marketing programme, or develop social media campaigns based on some great new marketing content delivered via social media? Which social media platform(s) will be prioritised? 'Sales promotion' has largely been replaced by 'content marketing' (free gifts of useful content). Content marketing may well be a major strategic component (assuming it supports the brand and the desired CX).

Engagement

There are different levels of visitor engagement. From encouraging visitors and customers to give ratings and reviews to nurturing advocates to collaborating and co-creating ideas and products. This is the Ladder Of Engagement starting with low level engagement (ratings and reviews) and at the top of the ladder is collaborative co-creation. You can download a complete chapter from the Welcome Page on PR Smith Marketing Facbook page. But also remember that not everyone wants to engage all the time, sometimes visitors just want to complete a task, find some information or just buy something and leave your site. So don't ignore the basics of properly tested, quick, easy-to-use websites and apps.

**Engagement boosts sales
- social media first-in wins**
Bain found that customers who engage with companies via social media channels spend 20- 40% more money with those companies than other customers. They also demonstrate a deeper emotional commitment to the companies, granting them an average 33 points higher NPS® (Net Promoter® Score)   (Barry et al. 2011)

**What about the X factor (or the CX factor)?
The customer experience is at the heart of your business and your strategy**
What a brand says about itself (through its brand positioning and brand propositions) is less important than the actual experience the brand delivers to its

customers across all touch-points. So although positioning and brand propositions are important they are less important than the actual customers' experiences (CX). The CX establishes the brand experience which needs to be clearly defined. CXM (Customer Experience Management) needs to be managed across functions, by all staff online and offline. So Positioning drives propositions which influence the CX. Some marketers define the CX along with the positioning and propositions. Others define them separately at the end and add them to their strategy. For those marketers the strategy acronym becomes TOPPP SITE X.

Costco v Apple customer experience
Costco customers expect bare-bones service in return for low prices, while Apple customers expect high quality innovative products at relatively high prices. Those are very different customer experiences, but they both delight customers (Brand & Hagen, 2011). And they are delivered to customers consistently online and offline.

Content marketing is hot – should it be no.1 component in your strategy?
If more than 85% of Google searches are for useful information and only 10% of searches are for products and services (Toll, 2014), it follows that producing good quality content will satisfy searchers' needs and give them a good experience. It also satisfies Googles new criteria for SEO which is basically relevant high quality content that people like

(and engage with) across multiple platforms (don't forget to put high quality content on your homepage too). You will see that Content Marketing is listed amongst 10 other tactical tools (in the Tactics section) but should it be number one? Well for companies like Red Bull it is. It is the driving force behind their marketing strategy.

Which tactical tool – content or PPC, email or search?
Should you spend more on Content Marketing than Paid Media? Or email or search? Or any of the other tools?

Some companies keep it simple, like Red Bull, spend most of their money on content that their demographic really wants. Red Bull recently released an 81 minute movie 'Where the Trail Ends' - this was after they had sponsored Red Bull Stratos - Mission to the Edge of Space and Supersonic Freefall parachute jump, which was made into a TV documentary complete with photo and video gallery and media tour. Red Bull content is simply excellent.

Can you become the Expert Wikipedia for your industry or topic whether it is B2B widgets or Red Bull?

People want high quality content. You can get more bangs for your content buck if you leverage it across all your comms mix.

So yes it is worth considering content marketing as the lead component in your digital marketing strategy, but remember it's competitive out there and there's a lot of other content competing for your customers' shortened attention spans.

Red Bull's contents support what their customers want and also the brand values. Source: Red Bull.

Customer retention or customer acquisition – a strategic decision

You must decide strategically which has priority: Customer Acquisition or Customer Retention (and therefore determine what resources will be allocated to each). We know customer retention is deemed to be, on average, six times more profitable than customer acquisition. It is therefore, generally speaking, worth investing in customer retention – that is if you have already acquired customers. This is part of the 'sequence' component of strategy (and arguably the Objectives component) and requires a strategic shift in thinking. See the Tactics section for three stunning tactical approaches (involving ads, sales promotions and CSR) once this major strategic decision is made.

Boardroom tip – watch the cash
Be clear about exactly how much resource your strategy requires. Your board will want to know exactly what resources are required – either budget or whether you have skilled people. Budgets don't always have to be included in a strategy, however mentioning budget , or 'S'pend keeps your presentation very grounded, i.e. forces marketers to at least announce what resources are required to deliver this strategy. So add another 'S' for Spend.

3.4 Sample Strategy Excerpts

Here are a selection of excerpts from digital marketing strategies. See if you can identify which strategic components from TOPPP SITES are being used.

Remember TOPPP SITES
Target markets; Objectives; Positioning; Partnerships; Processes; Sequence/Stages; Integration; Tactical Tools; Engagement Level; Spend/Budget.

Strategy Excerpt	TOPPP SITES
e.g. Unilever Switch budgets from online advertising spend to social media content across all product ranges.	Tactical Tools/Channels

TOPPP SITES Target markets; Objectives; Positioning; Partnerships; Processes; Sequence/Stages; Integration; Tactical Tools; Engagement Level; Spend/Budget.	TOPPP SITES
Twitter Developing the platform as a live TV companion, a new TV Guide or a new TV rating mechanism.	Positioning
GM Put $10 million into more traditional online advertising channels (search and display ads) and $30 million to maintain a Facbook presence and develop applications, to convert many of the brand's 3.9 million fans into brand advocates.	Tactical Tools (Channels) Engagement
MySpace New look website: features focused on music and connecting artists with fans becoming a key player in the music and entertainment industries.	Targeting Positioning Engagement

Target markets; Objectives; Positioning; Partnerships; Processes; Sequence/Stages; Integration; Tactical Tools; Engagement Level; Spend/Budget.	TOPPP SITES
Facbook (in specific developing countries) Position fb as 'The Internet' …Key to Facbook's strategy is …no matter where users start on the ladder of mobile technology, (from the most basic device to the newest smartphone), Facbook (which starts free) becomes better and more fun to use as they upgrade.	Positioning Targeting Engagement
HSBA Drive prospect traffic via a blend of inbound and outbound marketing via Automated Marketing and subsequently building incremental profiling via data profiling to ensure added value relevant offers and timely advice – reassure and reinvigorate customer relationships.	Tactical Tools (Channels) Integration (data) Process (Mktg Automation) Sequence

Target markets; Objectives; Positioning; Partnerships; Processes; Sequence/Stages; Integration; Tactical Tools; Engagement Level; Spend/Budget.	TOPPP SITES
RABODirect Grow fan base by engaging fans via social engagement through the development of a dynamic Twitter engagement tool called RaboScore complete with a leaderboard ranking the top 12 fans of the competition and use Gamification and online rewards to continually drive engagement particularly with key online influencers.	Tactical Tools (social + gamification) Engagement Targeting Sequence

3.5 Your Strategy Template

Your Strategy Template (simple version)
Summarise into a succinct (short) strategy statement:
Achieve ... sales and mkt share .... by
targeting......., positioned as.........

over a 1/2/3 stage campaign ......

using (list main tools including content strategy, PPC/SEO?)....

Partnering with.....Integrating customer data from....Marketing Automation and data Integration from social media to click behavioural (digital body language) to CRM and sales databases

Your TOPPP SITES Strategy Template
(comprehensive version)
Fill in and use whichever bits in whatever order feels
right – delete the rest

To achieve
....
sales (**Objectives**)
from ....(how many?) customers generating
............% market share from   by................(when)

by **Targeting** (target markets and personas)
....,

Positioned as
.... (crystal
clear positioning)
delivering ....(what
kind of a customer experience)
over .... (how many **Stages**
programme e.g. gaining endorsement from
influencers; generating awareness initially followed
by sales)
using ....(which main
Tactical Tools/channels (NB Content Marketing may
be a significant component – some strategies are
built around Content Marketing)

and **Partnering** with..
(are there any strategic partners that help you extend
your reach or add value to your proposition?)

and **Integrating** customer data ....
(which sources - both online and offline)

Using……………………………………………………………

(any new **Processes,** e.g. marketing automation, data integration from social media to click behaviour to CRM and sales databases to tailored canned messages or wrapping an automated and personalised contact 'strategy' around the customer lifetime journey….. or nurturing a data driven A/B culture of continuous improvement).

To **Engage**

…………………………………………………(prospects, customers and advocates)

at……………………………………….. (specify which level of engagement [low level: liking/sharing, ratings, reviews anddiscussions or collaborative co-creation] crowd sourcing ideas)………………………………………

Requiring a budget (**Spend**) of………………. (increasing or reducing in stages 1,2,and 3) and with a team of…………

Double-check the basics

Is customer experience in your strategy?
Remember a clearly defined customer experience is at the heart of your business (and ipso facto at the heart of your strategy). As mentioned, Positioning influences OVP which influences CX. Don't forget to define your CX.

Is content marketing in your strategy?

When you have written your first digital marketing strategy you will feel a little uncomfortable with it as it may well be your first time writing a digital marketing strategy. It does get easier. Basically you've now got some of the key components. You don't need to use them all, but do at least, consider each component to see if it can help to improve your strategy. Does it improve the big picture? Does it give clear direction and help to guide the selection of tactical tools?

Now try to develop a second strategy. A different strategy. There is more than one way to achieve the objectives. Some ways are better than others. You'll start to see this as you develop other alternative strategic options. Try to do this before selecting the best strategy. When you have your best strategy, you can use this next checklist to double check how good is your strategy.

Boardroom tip your biggest strategic challenge – change management

Getting your own business to buy into your strategy can sometimes prove too difficult. Given that many if not most, companies are dysfunctional and siloed to a greater or lesser degree, winning the business over to your new strategy (and getting them to understandit) is often a very challenging task, particularly if you are introducing some innovative ideas like combining your new 'content marketing' strategy with a new marketing automation process. Many of us have a neurotic resistance to change. So rehearse the logic of your new strategy and prepare for the typical Q and A that will follow your presentation. Do not take the criticism personally, it can be healthy and force you to check the robustness of your strategy.

> **'Great strategy but lousy execution'**
> **– don't accept this excuse!**
> There can never be 'a great strategy failing because of lousy execution' because the Situation Analysis will already have identified if capabilities (strengths and weaknesses) need to be improved.

3.6 Your Strategy Checklist

	Yes/No
1. Does your strategy seize opportunities to help customers even better via digital?' (Online value proposition)	
2. Does your strategy clearly address 'What Problem Am I Trying To Solve?' and then see if your strategy solves it.	
3. Does your strategy improve the customer experience?	
4. Does your strategy build relationships with customers and fans?	

5. Does your strategy strengthen your brand(s)?	
6. Does it create competitive advantage?	
7. Does it move with market trends?	
8. Are mobile, content marketing and social media part of your strategy?	
9. Do you have or, can you get, the resources required?	
10. Have you considered several strategic options before choosing this strategy?	

'All too often, the digital strategy discussion starts with "What's our social strategy?" or "What's our mobile strategy?" In the vast majority of cases, that has nothing to do with improving a business.' (Satell, 2012)

However, it's worth remembering that digital is only part of any solution/strategy since it is still 'people' who execute a strategy. See the Action section to discover how Action can help to execute tactics – the details of strategy. For now, however, let's consider Tactics (or tactical tools).

'Strategy without tactics
is the slowest route to victory.'
Sun Tzu, The Art of War

Chapter 4

Tactics

SOSTAC® is a registered trade mark of www.PRSmith.org

While strategy paints the bigger picture and ensures everything moves in the right direction, tactics are simply the details of strategy.

Which tactical tools will be used when, to achieve what and with how much budget etc.?

'Tactics without strategy is the noise before defeat.'
Sun Tzu, The Art of War

Tactical decisions are driven by the overarching strategy. A crystal clear positioning statement makes tactical decisions much easier.

As does clearly defined target markets and what you are trying to achieve with them (objectives).

There may even be a sequence or series of stages, perhaps some new processes (like marketing automation) and perhaps the challenge of integrating all of your customer data and prioritising tactical tools including marketing content.

In this Tactics section we get into the details of strategy.

4.1 Tactical Tools and The Marketing Mix

Tactics can cover the old Marketing Mix: product, price, place, promotion and the 'service mix' comprising people, processes and physical evidence.

However, digital blurs the lines and morphs the mix (e.g. social media is part of the product experience, promotional reach, physical evidence, and place/distribution).

Consider also 'Location Marketing'. It identifies customers with mobile phones in specific places and then offers special prices and promotions.

So here again, the old marketing mix is morphing since a single digital decision impacts several elements of the marketing mix.

So therefore let's focus on the Communications Mix (also known as the Promotional Mix which, is one of the original '4Ps' in the Marketing Mix) while acknowledging that detailed decisions about prices, product lines and distribution channels have to also be carefully considered.

Having said all that, a clear overarching digital marketing strategy guides these detailed tactical decisions.

4.2 Ten Tactical Tools - Offline and Online

1. Advertising	Interactive ads, pay per click keyword, display ads, remarketing/retargeting
2. Public Relations	Online editorial, newsletters, ezines, discussion groups, viral marketing, vine
3. Sponsorship	Sponsoring online events/sites service
4. Sales Force/ Agents/Tele-Marketing	Virtual sales staff, affiliate marketing, web rings, links/chat
5. Exhibitions, Events and Conferences	Virtual exhibitions, virtual events, webinars
6. Direct Mail	Opt-in email and eNewsletter
7. Retail Store or Office HQ	Website (seo and marketing automation opportunity)
8. Word Of Mouth	Recommendations, criticisms, feedback

	devices (e.g. reevoo.com), social media platforms, forums
9. Sales Promotion	Content Marketing, incentives, rewards, online loyalty schemes, competitions
10. Merchandising and Packaging	e-tailing, QR Codes, augmented reality, virtual reality. NB real packaging must be displayed online

4.3 Ten Tactical Tools Primary Objectives

There are exceptions to these generalisations, e.g. advertising can build positive attitudes and preference as well as building awareness.

Exhibitions are often used to establish a presence (or build awareness – 'we have to be there since competition is there'), however I argue that there may be more cost-effective ways to build awareness.

Hence I've simplified the purpose or objectives of each tactical tool listed below.

At the very least this table may generate a discussion regarding which tools will do what for your organisation.

10 Tactical Tools	Primary Objectives
1. Advertising	Awareness (and credibility)
2. Public Relations	Awareness (and credibility/reputation)
3. Sponsorship	Awareness (and credibility and sampling)
4. Sales Force/ Agents/Tele-Marketing	Sales (and relationship building and gathering information)
5. Exhibitions, Events and Conferences	Sales (and relationship building and gathering information)
6. Direct Mail	Sales (and relationship building and gathering information)
7. Retail Store /Office HQ/Hub	Relationship building, database building, identifying prospects, enquiries, sales, CRM
8. Word Of Mouth	Awareness, Credibility (including endorsements and recommendations), Conversions
9. Sales Promotion	Conversion (enquiry/lead/newsletter/sale, post-sale relationship)
10. Merchandising and Packaging	Conversion and relationship building

The preceding objectives are somewhat oversimplified. Advertising is used to build awareness. It can also be used to reassure existing buyers that they are buying the right brands in the case of car advertisements. PPC ads (and even display ads) can also arouse sufficient interest that a percentage of the audience will click through to a website or a social media platform to eventually convert (whether this is registering for a newsletter, making an enquiry, trying a sample, buying a product or engaging with content that strengthens the ongoing relationships).

Gamification – Strategy or Tactics?
Is gamification a tactical tool? I tend to categorise it as a sales promotion (and therefore a tactical tool) whether it is aimed at customers, employees, distributors or any other stakeholder. See Gamification The Good , The Bad and The Ugly (on www.prsmith.org/blog for more.

Real Time Marketing – Strategy or Tactics?
'Real Time Marketing' is an exciting buzz word. RTM has several interpretations including:

- Quick release/reaction marketing to external current events and cultural happenings – usually ads.

- Quick release/reaction marketing that finds a way to inject its brand as relevant in a conversation – social media news-jacking.

- Marketing that automatically delivers dynamic, personalised content across multichannels (marketing automation) triggered by click behaviour, purchase behaviour, a buyer's buying cycle, or a sequence of contacts (including email).

Are these strategic or tactical? It is strategic if a decision is made to allocate a team of three agency staff to monitor social media discussions and hot news and generate new ideas for release each day for the next six months. Many events are predictable and can be planned for whilst leaving budget for the unpredictable event – this would be a strategic approach. Simply reacting to a one-off opportunity would be more tactical. The classic Oreo biscuits tweet when the Superbowl suffered a blackout generated huge coverage (Watercutter, 2013).

When the Superbowl XLVII had an electrical blackout a rapid response tweet from the Oreo Twitter account caught the nation's imagination and became massively popular; an excellent piece of real-time marketing.

4.4 Which Tactical Tools Should You Use?

One of the big decisions, 'which tactical tools to use'
is partially answered by the objectives already set.
Building awareness is often best done by advertising,
PR and Sponsorship, while converting awareness, or
ideally preference, into sales can require direct mail
(email and/or snail mail), websites (with strong calls
to action) and/or sales people (face to face, online or
virtual) in retail stories, on the street or at events.

Each of these tools should be supported with some
relevant sales promotion whether this a gift or some
useful marketing content to help to convert the
prospect to the next stage. Again there are, of
course, exceptions.

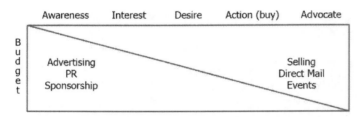

Splitting the marketing budget depending on what your objective is
e.g. awareness or selling (B2C)

You can see that in business-to-consumer (B2C)
markets if you need to build awareness you spend
more on ads, PR and sponsorship. If you already
have a level of awareness you can spend more
converting this into sales by more expenditure on
selling, direct mail (and email) and events,
conferences and exhibitions. There are of course,
exceptions. Some ads are designed to sell directly,

or at least drive traffic to a website or even to a telemarketing team that will complete the sale.

Customer retention tactics v customer acquisition tactics

Your digital marketing strategy will have identified which has priority: Customer Acquisition or Customer Retention (and therefore determine what resources will be allocated to each).

A customer's LTV (Life Time Value) might be worth sales of say, 20 cars or 50 mobile phones (during the customer's life). Obviously this is worth a lot more than selling one car or one mobile and hence why customer retention is deemed to be, on average, 6 times more profitable than customer acquisition. It is therefore, generally speaking, worth investing in customer retention.

Let's assume you have identified retention as part of the strategy. Once a company embraces this idea the culture becomes more customer-centric, and part of this is carefully anticipating and planning when a customer is due to move back into the repeat buying cycle, so marketers can optimise their offers at precisely the right time and block out competition with timely and relevant service.

Here are three stunning customer retention examples using different tactics from sales promotions, to ads, to CSR (Corporate Social Responsibility Programmes) – all three also integrate with social media tactics. Sit back and enjoy these amazing tactical approaches to taking care of your existing customers (and getting some publicity for it).

1. Ulster Rugby
Rewards some customers for renewing their season tickets by giving them the very personal touch (a beautiful customer experience) which makes great social media content, which in turn spreads awareness, affection, liking and maybe further down the road opens up the opportunity to convert some more sales. Here's Some 'Wow' Customer Retention! (see the video, and post, about customer retention at www.prsmith.org/blog).

Customer Retention Isn't Boring with Ulster Rugby

2.. Sports Club Recife
Now this is a truly unique approach to customer retention by Brazilian football club Sport Club Recife who reinforced their club's community feeling by launching an organ donor campaign. Some call this a CSR programme (Corporate Social Responsibility). It strengthens the real community feeling that fans experience when they follow a club passionately.

Driven by the club's Facbook page, some leaflets and posters, the club now has 51,000 donors (the stadium only holds 41,000) with waiting lists for hearts, lungs and eyes eradicated. See how excited the fans are about this CSR programme.

See this stunning video in the same post 'Wow Customer retention' on www.prsmith.org/blog

3. TD Bank

TD bank in Canada turned ATMs into Automated Thanking Machines™ to create some very special moments for customers across the country. A simple thank you can change someone's day. #TDThanksYou adds a personalised gift to it and people get very happy.

This is 'psychic income', e.g. two tickets to a baseball game cost, say, $90. If you give someone $90 cash it won't be remembered or loved as much as two tickets to see a baseball game. Why? Because this addresses Maslow higher level needs – transcendental/self actualisation. Add a relevant gift and people get ecstatic.

See TD's Automated Thinking Machine™ in action on www.prsmith.org/blog 'Wow customer retention'..

See this emotional video in the same post 'Wow Customer retention' on www.prsmith.org/blog

In each case the organisation owns the media (the video) and they can post it on their 'owned channels', i.e. on their own youtube channel, Facbook, google+, Twitter stream, website and other social media platforms. This is 'owned media'. If they decide to 'promote' a post or a tweet, this is 'paid media' as is any form of paid advertising. Any engagement (Likes, shares, comments) is earned by the quality of the content – hence called 'earned media'.

Choosing which tactics - owned, earned and paid media

Owned Media includes your own website andyour own social media platforms. Earned Media is the interactions, the engagement or conversations you earn on your platforms (or elsewhere) from good quality content, while Paid Media is what it says on the tin – advertising which includes both PPC ads and banner ads. Paid Placements (paying to promote your posts and tweets) has now also become part of effective social media tactics.

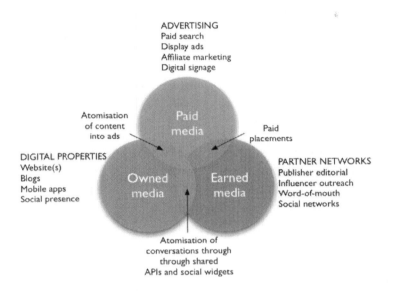

Chaffey and Chadwick (2013)

Owned, Earned and Paid Media – the free ride is over for 'Owned'

Owned, Earned and Paid Media can be integrated, particularly as social media platforms like Facbook are reducing organic reach and forcing marketers to pay for posts to reach wider audiences (paid placements). As Marko Muellner (2013) said 'To influence significant numbers of people via social streams, you need to aggregate large fan communities and then, in many cases, pay per post or share, to increase your campaign scope to existing fans, friends of fans, and beyond. Successful social media advertising requires integrated strategies that consider how organic, earned, and paid media work with content and interactivity to drive outcomes. They are all inexorably intertwined and must be planned and executed accordingly.' For more, see 'The Rise and Fall Of Owned Earned and Paid Media' on www.prsmith.org/blog.

Atomisation means breaking content into micro assets or bite size chunks (some of which is done automatically through APIs, e.g. posting on a blog automatically triggers a Facbook announcement which in turn triggers a tweet. You can see how easily a survey can be repurposed into an book and then broken into a series of posts, tweets, videos, and infographics.

Owned, Earned and Paid Media can influence a prospect/customer at various stages of their buying journey. Paid Media is effective at generating awareness and perhaps preference or consideration amongst your target audience, while Earned Media is powerful at helping your prospects and customers to build loyalty and eventually become advocates. Owned Media can help to build consideration as well as deliver a positive customer experience.

Here's a different way of looking at how these tactical tools (Owned, Earned and Paid) affect the brand experienced by the customer/prospect on his or her journey towards a purchase. This next graphic is from ZenithOptimedia and it shows the consequences of activitaing a particular type of media (channel or tactical tool) on the journey towards purchasing.

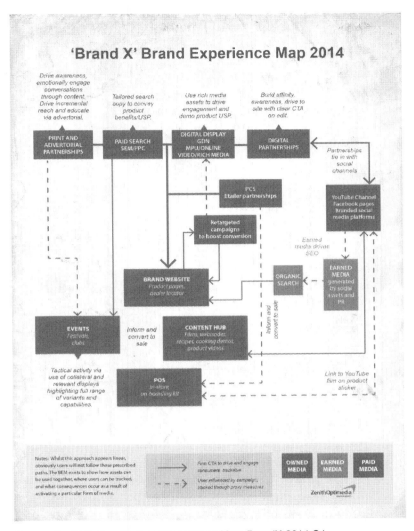

Source: ZenithOptimedia BrandExperience Map: BrandX 2014 Q1

For more on Owned, Earned and Paid see my post, The Rise and Fall Of Owned and Earned But Not Paid Media – World Cup Marketing Wars (www.prsmith.org/blog). Or if you want to see five different viewpoints try this, 'The difference between paid, owned and earned media – 5 viewpoints' on SmartInsights.com.

The Free Ride Is Over (for Owned Media)
Social Media Marketing always required great content, carefully seeded into the right influencers, at the right time and shared with your own audience which you built carefully. Today brands spend cash 'to reach an audience that someone else invested many millions to create'… today you have to 'pay to play' (but you pay a lot less if you have great content). The 'free' (it was never quite free anyway) ride for brands on Facbook is coming to an end, and Facbook should now be moved into the 'paid channel' in the marketing budget. (See Bosomworth 2014 for how to respond to the decline in Facbook organic reach).

4.5 Which Tactical Tools -The Tactical Matrix

This is another way of deciding which tactical tools to use. Assuming you are clear about what objectives you are you are trying to achieve, I'm going to show you my Tactical Matrix which is designed to trigger some discussion about which tactical tool is best for you. Firstly we look at how good each tactic is at moving your prospects/customers through various stages of the Lifetime Buying Process (note this is another variation on some of the other buying models, or stages of buying):

- Awareness

- Consideration

- Purchase

- Post-Purchase Relationship Building

- Post-Purchase Repeat Sales

The need for segmenting your customers or prospects by stage of the buying process emerges again. Now, depending on what stage of the buying cycle you are trying to move your prospects/customers through, you can consider how good each tactic is across these 9 criteria:

1. Reach (how big an audience can it reach?)

2. Speed (how quickly can it reach that audience?)

3. Time (how long to create and deliver this tactic?)

4. Message Volume (space to fit message in?)

5. Targeting (how granular or precise can the targeting be?)

6. Personalisation (can the tool personalise messages?)

7. Cost – is it expensive on a Cost Per Thousand (CPT/CPM) basis?

8. Control – can you control the message with this tactic?

9. Credibility – some tactics have more credibility.

Tactics Matrix	BENEFIT →	Reach	Speed	Lead Time	Message Size	Targeting	Personal-ization	Cost CPC/CPM	Control	Credibility (message)
OBJECTIVE ↓	**TACTIC/ CHANNEL ↓**									
Awareness/ Familiarity	Display Ads	High	Medium	Long / Med	Medium	High	Medium	Medium	Medium	Low
	PR	High	Medium	Medium	Large	Low	Low	Low	Low	High
	Sponsorship	High	Low/Med	Long	Small	Low	Low	Medium	Low	Medium
	Social media (content marketing)	Low/Med High	Low / Med	Medium	Large	Medium	Med / Low	None	Low / Med	High
Consideration	Search Ads & SEO	Low/Med	Medium	Long/Med	Small	High	Medium	Medium	High	Low / Med
	eMail (AM)	Med	High	Short	Large	High	High	Low	High	Medium
	Web Site Incentives	Low/Med	Low	Medium	Med / Low	Low/Med	High with Auto Marketing	None	High	Medium
	Social Media	Low/Med /High	Low	Short / Med	Large	Medium	Med / Low	None	Low / Med	High
	Sales Pitch	Low	Medium	Short	N/A	High	High	High	High	Med / High
Decision	Search Ads & SEO	Med / Low	Medium	Short	Small	High	Medium	Medium	High	Low / Med
	eMail (AM)	Medium	High	Short	Large	High	High	Low	High	Medium
	Web Site Incentives	Low	Low	Medium	Low	N/A	High with Auto Marketing	N/A	High	N/A
	Telesales	Low/Med	High	Short / Med	Large	High	High	Low	High	Medium
	Sales Pitch	Low	Medium	Short	Low	High	High	High	High	Med / High
	Exhibition	Medium	Medium	Med/Long	Large	High	Low	High	Medium	Med / High
Post Purchase Relationship Building	Direct Mail/email newsletter/ special offers added value	Medium	High	Short (eM) Med (Dmail)	Large	High	High	Low (eMail) High (DM)	High	Medium
	Social Media	Low/High	Low	Short/Med	Large	High	Medium	None	Low / Med	High
Post Purchase Repeat Sales Loyalty. Adv.	Direct Mail/eMail	Medium	High	Med/Short	Large	High	High	High (DM)	High	Medium
	Social Media	Low/High	Med	Short/Med	High	High	Medium	None	Low / Med	High

The Tactics Matrix www.PRSmith.org © PR Smith 2014 v2

The Tactics Matrix: you can download this graphic and enlarge it or share it wth colleagues from the Tactics Matrix excerpt on my www.PRSmith.org/blog

The last 3 criteria (cost, control and credibility) are sometimes used initially when choosing which tactical tool to employ. We know that some tools give you more control over your message (advertising as opposed to PR or even social media), while some tools cost a lot more (direct mail v advertising) in cost per thousand reached (NB they compare a bit better when looking at cost per eventual conversion). And some tools have more Credibility, e.g. PR, or editorial, has arguably three times more credibility than advertising in the UK while thousands of reviews on social media have, for many, the most credibility.

So this Tactical Matrix tries to encapsulate all of this – the 10 comms tools, the 5 stages of the buying process and the 9 criteria to help you to choose which tactical tool is best for your plan. It was developed with the assistance of Mohamad Sameh, marketing manager of ITV Agency, Cairo.

I apologise that this is probably difficult to read here in this book but you can download it here from my PRSmith Marketing Blog. It is something of work in progress, designed to help marketers discuss different criteria when choosing between different tactical tools (or channels). I welcome all comments.

.

.

4.6 Which Tactical Tools and When

Clearly defined objectives will also help you to decide how to spend your marketing budget (as mentioned, ads, PR and Sponsorship are good at raising awareness, while Selling, Direct Mail and Events were better tactical tools for closing sales). There are of course exceptions to all of these as social media conversations and reviews (earned media) can create some awareness and certainly help convert visitors to sales and even onto becoming advocates. Here's a Tactics Gantt chart summarising what happens when (and how much is spent).

The Gantt Chart on the next page shows a bird's eye view of which tactical tools happen when and for how much

So you have to decide which tactical tools (or channels) to allocate your resources to (and when). and within each tactical tool you have to choose which vehicle or, in the case of social media, which particular social media platform? In some cases you will face tough questions such as, 'Should I spend more on Facbook or not?' (particularly as Facbook now wants you to pay to promote your posts). See 'Should I increase or reduce my Facbook budget?' later.

Which Tactical Tools When (& how much budget)

	J	F	M	A	M	J	J	A	S	O	N	D	€/$
Web Site	x	x											25k
Forums			x	x	x	x			x	x	x	x	5k
Social Media			xxxx	xxxx	xxxx	xxxx	x	x	xxxx	xxxx	xxxx	xxxx	30k
SEO	x		x		x		x		x		x	x	15k
Advertising													
Display/Banner Ads		x							x	x	x		15k
Pay Per Click Ads			x			x			x			x	20k
Facbook Ads													40k
Twitter Ads													10k
Sponsorship	x	x	x	x	x	x	x	x	x	x	x	x	10k
Online sponsorship – communities, pages, sites, events													
Public Relations News Releases			x		x		x	x	x		x		10k
Viral Marketing						x	x						
Direct Mail													
Opt-In eMail (NB retention v acquisition)				x			x			x			20k
Sales Promotion/Competition emails, web sites & social media			x			x			x		x		10k
Agency: Market Prospecting			x	x	x	x	x	x	x	x	x	x	
Affiliate & Partner Marketing										x	x	x	20k
Exhibitions & Events													50k
Virtual Exhibitions, Virtual worlds like Second Life										x			20k
Total													300k

Marketing Communications Gantt Chart

The good news is that your analytics makes these decisions a lot easier as it enables you to make more informed decisions about which tactical tools (channels) are delivering you the best results.

Your analytics tells you where your traffic is coming from, which tactical channel (ads, SEO, email, links, social media etc.) even which social media channel. So if you get more visitor traffic from, say, Facbook on a particular topic or type of content it may be worthwhile spending some budget promoting these type of posts to get even more traction- particularly if the visitors from these sources actually convert to registrations, enquiries or sales. More on Analytics (and multichannel funnel analytics) in the 'Control' section.

Which social media channel? - go where the conversations are

On which channels do most of your customers spend time conversing? Identify where your target audience is communicating about your brand, your competitors and other relevant topics. If most of your customers' discussions are on LinkedIn and not Twitter, you should invest more resources on LinkedIn.

Should you invest more in Facbook or not?

What questions would you ask if you were the marketing manager of a ski holiday company, - Crystal Ski - and you were trying to decide whether it was worth investing more in Facbook or not? What specific questions would you want answering?

Remember 'Who, Why and How' might help you. Look away for a few moments and think about what questions you would ask. You can see the full case in an excellent post in Smart Insights.

For now, here are the initial 5 questions:
1. Are you a customer and, if yes, how much do you buy each year?
2. Why do you like our Facbook page *(competition/prizes; offers; tips and insights; contact us)*
3. *After seeing our brand's content in your news feed did you ever feel better about our brand; visit our website; consider buying; buy; tell a friend?*
4. How likely would you be to recommend our brand or share the Facbook page?
5. How likely would you be to recommend us to friends and family?

Read this full intriguing example of how ski holiday company, Crystal Ski, asked (and got answers to) some great questions which determined if their Facbook page was worthwhile. See 'Searching For The Real Value Of Facbook Marketing' on the Smart Insights website .

Should you keep developing your brand on Facbook?
How much marketing resource, if any, should you allocate to Facbook? If most of your customers and target prospects are using Facbook, then it is likely to be 'yes spend more'. The reverse is likely to be true too: if none of them have migrated to Facbook, then don't bother spending money on Facbook. So firstly,

check to see what percentage of your actual customers and target prospects use Facbook. Does your Facbook page introduce, influence or convert sales (in 'attribution models' language this means what role does a particular channel, like Facbook, have in the customers' path to conversion)? After that, you might want to carry out a survey of your existing Facbook fans covering the types of questions listed above.

Why are your average sales via Facbook lower than via the website?
In the Crystal Ski case, the average revenue dropped by 18% if the path to conversion included Facbook.

Lots of reasons could explain this, the obvious one being that the occasional flash sales the brand runs, reduces the average price of a holiday bought by customers using this channel . So you can learn a lot about your community by asking just a few good questions.

4.7 Tactical Targeting - More Bang For Your Buck

Customer profiling helps tactical targeting
The success of your tactics is partly dependent upon how good your targeting skills are.

It is worth spending time considering carefully what is your ideal customer profile(s) and how you might find more of them using a variety of new tools available.

Detailed customer profiling makes it easier to find more customers when you:
- Target direct mail and email via databases with similar types of customers.
- Target ads at very specific customer profiles.
- Target social selling at very specific customer profiles.

Target similar customer profiles - direct mail

You can find similar 'ideal customer profiles' by inserting (or 'indexing') the attributes of your best customers (or even just the attributes of the best converters on your site) to find additional ideal prospects from external third party databases like Net Mining' and Adjug Ad Exchange . They profile your customers and then give you similar ones from their own databases. Today, a clever question can deliver really hot prospects from a previously untapped database such as WEVE (the new mobile network database). See 'Who are the frequent flyers?' in a few minutes.

Target very specific customer profiles - ads

You can now target very specific audiences. For example, on Facbook, you can find prospects with similar preferences as your own customers ('lookalikes'). Then target by location (country, state, city, postcode); networks (people whose friends are connected to your page, people already connected); interests (business, hobbies, fitness/wellness, entertainment) and right down to games, movies or the music they like; behaviour (travel, mobile device, digital activities); demographics (age, gender, language and education, generation, work, relationship status) and a lot more.

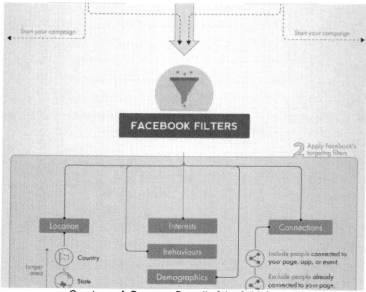

Courtesy of Qwaya – See all of the full infographic.
on Qwaya.com

Both Facbook and LinkedIn allow you to target ads and/or promoted posts by interests, age, geographic locations and a lot more (as shown in the many Facbook 'filters').

Or you can target specific types of visitors to your web site (customers that visit certain pages can be retargeted with specific and relevant ads after they have left your site as they mover around other sites that are within the same advertising network (e.g. Google Ads network).

Target prospects talking about xyz via social media and third party databases

Companies like clever-touch.com have developed a micro IP proprietary programme that searches intelligently for relevant B2B prospects who are talking about, or expressing interest in, specific products, services, problems, issues, challenges or opportunities. People who hashtag a particular word or acronym (adding # before a word or acronym) flag the word up as important in their discussion so that anyone else can easily join the conversation 'thread' about the hashtagged word. Drawing on major third party database owners and searching across social media platforms, these people can be quickly identified and filtered by country, language, company type, company size and even an individual's interest.

Target prospects talking about any key topics and feed to sales reps

Social Monitoring Streams can be set up for each sales rep with a list of their leads. They are immediately notified when any of these leads mention your company name, or any of the topics mentioned above. See Hubspot's 6 Ways Social Data Can Inform Your Marketing Strategy (and Tactics).

Who are the frequent flyers who might take a train instead?

If you were trying to sell train tickets to frequent flyers - who are the ideal prospects? Your ability to ask great questions, find databases and interrogate them

---

in new ways to profile prospects is a great skill. Look away. Stop and think for a moment.

How about asking data owners of major mobile networks (e.g. WEVE) to find 'mobile users who disappear in Heathrow and reappear in Edinburgh in the time a flight would take'. Then segment these travellers and promote highly relevant offers via their mobiles. Add a mobile commerce component enabling prospects to directly purchase a rail ticket, or just wave their smartphone at the ticket counter or transport kiosk. (SAS, 2014) Could mobile technologies be the future of retail?

Target event attendees talking # and feed to automated marketing

You can find prospects in a particular conversation, e.g. delegates' tweets at conferences or events usually include the conference or event hashtag. Instead of buying that expensive attendees list from the organiser, run a 60 second search for a conference hashtag in CrowdVu.com and get email, phone and social data – which can be further filtered by geographic region, e.g. a search for anyone tweeting about #InfoSec (the Information Security Technical Conference) delivers a delegate list of 1,104 delegates' email addresses, job titles, locations, company sizes (via a 'matching engine' that cross references and checks against other databases and social platforms with 95% accuracy). An automated marketing campaign can then target tailored relevant information to this hot target list.

Hashtags **How interest in one topic may translate into interest in another**

People group topics together so it's useful to see what topics/key phrases relate to each other. Hashtagify.me website shows you what hashtags are being used in conjunction with one another. How interest in one topic may translate to another. (Murphy, 2013). This site (followerwonk) identifies influencers for any hashtag and also searches for common interests with these influencers making it easier to connect with them.

Target specific prospects via instigating conversation - social selling

After clearly defining the 'ideal customer' profile, set up a new LinkedIn page, register as a LinkedIn Pro and using Boolean coding, carefully target and invite, say, 300 prospects p.c.m. to join highly relevant discussions (for their specific industry sector).

Say, on average 100+ join. Phase 2 roll starts some good conversations. Phase 3 invites members for a 1-2-1 skype chat re: specific solutions that the prospect is interested in. This can generate up to ten highly qualified leads p.c.m. Some marketers believe social media is about helping and not about selling; I feel it is down to how relevant and useful the discussions are. It all comes back to helping the customer.

Target specific prospects by social interests, technologies or skills

Prospects can also be targeted via their enterprise systems, e.g. show me contacts from all companies who are using a particular technology (say 'Salesforce'), who are located in London, where contacts have a job function of marketing or sales at a senior level (director) and are interested in sales and marketing alignment. This might only produce a small list of prospects but it can be a valuable list of hot prospects. Once you find them, then engage with these contacts on a highly personalised level, either via email, direct mail, telephone or on social media.

Target better quality visitors with seo

Sometimes conversion rates are low because you may be attracting the wrong type of visitor. Perhaps less volume of visitors but better quality of visitors can improve your situation. I mentioned the importance of Search Engine Optimisation in chapter 1 and it is worth remembering that although high quality SEO will get you more visitors by being listed high up in search engine results pages (SERPS) for phrases that your ideal customers are using, it does require a budget.

The SEO budget may be spread as some companies there is a joint responsibility for SEO and social media marketing since SEO today is more dependent on good quality content and social media marketing than the technical aspects of SEO. However, ignoring SEO may mean that 'competitors will be eating your lunch via Google' (source unknown).

Targeting influencers

If you are opening a sushi restaurant in New York – you can find the most influential sushi Twitter users within a radius of 10 miles and then start interacting with them. Analyse your members' interests – then personalise your messages.

See what the best time to tweet is. What topics are most popular with them? Then target this list with a DM campaign (direct message via Twitter). You can also do this with your competitor's community – tracking their followers every day. Or do this with the whole Twitter community or with those that tweet with a particular hashtag or even just a word, or a link.

Tweetreach measures the total number of impressions generated by tweets, who saw them and who helped to spread the word. Tweetreach uses advertising language such as reach and impressions.

Other tools like SocialBro cover some of the 'Who, Why and How' questions including: who has followed and unfollowed you? Who are your influencers - listed according to level of influence, location, gender, how active they are on Twitter? I've mentioned followerwonk.com which also identifies influencers that are following you, or you can just create a list of influencers in your Twitter account.

One of many social media dashboards, Hootsuite, helps you to monitor and converse with multiple social platforms including Facbook, LinkedIn, Twitter and more via a single dashboard.

*Blogger Outreach Programmes identify and work with Opinion Formers. See digital guru Zaid Al Zaidy, talking about how agencies use 'Blogger Outreach' programmes.

Zaid Al Zaidy talking about Blogger Outreach Programmes on Youtube PRSmith1000 channel

4.8 The Magic Marketing Formula

Whichever tactical tools (or channels) you use and whether manual or automated communications, always apply the Magic Marketing Formula - IRD - to boost results.

- Identify needs.
- Reflect these needs (through ads, sales presentations, search engines etc.)

- Deliver a good customer experience (i.e. fulfil your promise consistently at every touch point).

If Coca Cola identify that people need to be loved, they reflect this by showing ads of people drinking Coke and having a good time (whether polo bears or people); there is a good feeling that love exists. If a B2B IT supplier identifies a segment's main need is, say, security, then it reflects 'security' in its ads, exhibitions, social media and optimises for these key phrases.

A simpler example is obvious with the search engines and the magic marketing formula when you search for a very specific multi-word key phrase and then you see the exact phrase appear in the Search Engine results. It is a eureka moment. It's like a fusion of your specific need with a supplier's offering. The perfect match. This is the formula reflecting your needs (phrases) through SEO.

A shocking example of the Magic Marketing Formula

Here's a shocking example of the Magic Marketing Formula in action. Road deaths from speeding drivers is an issue in Northern Ireland. In-depth research by the Department of the Environment, revealed that speeders feel it is their right to drive at whatever speed they want.

They won't change this for anything. 'What about if you killed someone?' No this would not stop them. 'What about if you killed a child?' A resounding chilling silence. The idea was born. These shocking ads reflected the horror of killing a child.

A shockvertisement that stops drivers from speeding

The ad went viral. Millions are watching it. Speeders are slowing down. With the economic cost of a death estimated at £1.68m and the campaign cost of £400,000 you can see that this ad can be justified on a purely economic basis.

On an emotional basis you might find this disturbing, but it does increase awareness and, most importantly, change behaviour. In fact, AdWeek praised the 60 second ad for "driving the anti-speeding message into the public conversation far beyond Ireland."

You can see this shocking ad, how it went viral and the research that went into it on Research Driven Shock Ad Uses Magic Formula and Goes Viral at www.prsmith.org/blog.

Do Not Be Afraid

'Brands must not be afraid to fail early and often, as this accelerates the chance of being successful. In this process, speed is the key. Success isn't linear; instead, it encompasses a multitude of decision points, with which we must experiment early, fail early, and reap the rewards from an iterative methodology. There must be continual optimization at every part of the marketing process for continued and repeatable success.' (Hudson, 2014)

The challenge – moving from campaigns to customer life cycles

The challenge, it seems, is to somehow move away from campaigns to conversations. In fact continuing conversations across owned, earned and paid media. This is particularly true if the buying cycle lasts longer than the campaign period. It is also true of the Northern Ireland ad campaign. How they somehow continue to stay front of mind. There lies the ongoing challenge after the initial 60 second success! Marketing Automation can help here.

Constant conversations, content marketing and marketing automation

In the quest for constant relevant conversation with both existing customers and prospects, 24/7, 365 days of the year, marketing automation has a role to play, particularly if there is a stream of relevant and interesting content being produced. We will look at the actual process required to develop great content and develop your marketing automation in the Action section.

Email behavioural responses such as 'opens' (of the email) and 'click-throughs' (to the links in the email) are also recorded so that those that don't open the email might get a second email with a different message in the subject line and those that did open the email but didn't click through might get a completely different second email message.

Effectively, every visit and every interaction online can be added over time to learn more about the customer, progressively improve the visitor's profile and automatically deliver more relevant content.

If the marketing automation is given a good set of rules – rules that continually identify the prospect's developing needs, then the content automatically given to the prospect actually reflects their needs.

Continuously striving to improve this process, embraces the Magic Marketing Formula. For example a mail shot invites prospects to download a white paper. Those that respond submit their industry sector in the form. The next email offers a free report on the recipient's own specific industry sector.

So there are many existing and new tactical tools to help marketers. Now let us explore the execution of the tactics in the chapter called 'Actions'.

Chapter 5

Actions

SOSTAC® is a registered trade mark of www.PRSmith.org

Strategy summarises, and gives direction to, 'How you are going to get there?' Tactics are the details of strategy and Action is the details of tactics. The Action section of your plan ensures that the tactics are executed to the highest possible standard.

The Action section includes:
- Systems
- Processes
- Guidelines
- Checklists
- Internal Marketing

All of these help to ensure high quality execution.

Internal Marketing is largely about internal communications and motivation to make sure everyone understands what the marketing activities are all about and everyone knows who has to do what, when and how. This can include mini action plans since each tactic is a mini project which needs professional execution. You don't have to include all the mini projects in the initial plan.

You can add systems, processes, guidelines and checklists, either into the body of the plan or in the appendices at the back, or you can simply issue them later. The Action section of your plan is about ensuring that your plan is executed to a high standard.

"Everything degenerates into work."
Peter Drucker

How many major brands deliver sloppy website experiences?

How many brands do not execute their plans to a high standard? How much money is wasted driving traffic to a website that frustrates visitors? 'Develop credibility before raising visibility', i.e. do website usability testing before promoting the site.

In this case, lousy execution not only wastes scarce resources but also destroys the customer experience and hence destroys the brand. The ad spend is destroying the brand!

Excellent Execution = Competitive Advantage

If you execute strategy and tactics better than your competitors you can create competitive advantage - just through better Action/Execution. A former CEO of GE and a Harvard Business Professor actually wrote a book claiming that an organisation's ability to execute (better than their competitors) generates competitive advantage. They called it "Execution: The discipline of getting things done", by Larry Bossidy and Ram Charan (2012).

'Vision without execution is just hallucination.'
Henry Ford

To help to execute each tactic it helps if the tactic has its own detailed objectives, an allocated budget, a list of who does what, when and ideally, an estimate of the return generated by the tactic – whether this is sales generated, number of visitors, level of engagement (number of Likes, shares, comments) or even level of awareness generated or level of preference generated. You can put a financial value on each of these including awareness levels (greater awareness = greater market share), the value of a Like, even just a visit or moving prospects through the funnel (e.g. from home page to product demonstration).

This is good practice and you can see how tactics, action and control start to overlap. SOSTAC ® is just an easy-to-remember, logical structure for the sections of your plan. Adjust it as you see fit.
So this Action section is designed to ensure better quality execution. This includes:
- Objectives, budget, responsibilities and an estimate of the return
- Systems and processes (e.g. content marketing production; marketing automation; database analysis)
- Guidelines (e.g. social media guidelines; brand guidelines)
- Checklists (e.g. to boost conversions; to increase credibility)
- Constant small improvements
- Motivation and training (silos, training, motivation, communication)

I'll spend a little more time on the processes involved in both Content Marketing and also Marketing Automation as they are two 'hot' topics right now.

Both can be significant components in your strategy. So I will briefly show you the 'actions' required to make these happen. We'll cover the other four subsections with a few short paragraphs.

5.1 Mini Action Plans

When executing each tactic it helps to keep everyone focused on doing a good job if the tactic has its own detailed objectives, a budget, responsibilities and estimated returns.

Here are two examples of how tactics cascade down into actions and details. One is from a Facbook ad campaign and the other from a Twitter ad campaign (both are from Smart Insights 'Party Central Plan').

Facbook Ad Campaign

Tactic	Objective	Action	Who	When	Budget
Facbook ad campaign	Increase traffic from 250,000 unique visitors per month to 400,000 pcm over a 12 month period.	Sign up for Facbook ads, select specific products to use for promoted stories and trial for one month	Dig Mktg Mngr	April 2015	£50,000

The Facbook page includes a 'new products' section and our Google Analytics shows us that this drives an average of 1,000 new sales to our website each month (1%). Whilst this is low, these are higher spending visitors with an average spend of £150. They particularly buy the 'colour sets' (e.g. coral earrings, matching necklace and bangles) and 30% opt for the express delivery service.

For ads, we're estimating a £1.12 cost per click with a 0.5% clickthrough rate and a lower average basket of £40. This indicates we exceed our £800k target, but as this is a trial, we will need to adjust after month 1.

Media	Bud-get £	Estim ated cost per click	Click-throu gh rate %	Pot-ential reach	Click-through s	Aver-age baske t £	Sales gen-erated £
Face-book	25000	1.12	0.5	4464286	22321	40	892857

This will cover the cost of the campaign and generate additional likes, which will in turn, generate further sales.

Twitter Ad Campaign

Tactic	Objective	Action	Who	When	Budget
Twitter ad campaign	Drive17,000 more visitors to the website to generate £600,000 sales	Sign up for Twitter ads, select specific products to use for promoted tweets and trial for one month	Dig Mktg Mngr	May 2015	£15,000

Twitter Ad Campaign

Google Analytics shows us that Twitter drives an average of 10% new visitors to our website each month. So 35,000 fans deliver 3,500 visitors a month, with a higher conversion rate of 1% (they will be shown an image before clicking) and a higher spend rate (£72 per basket).

Our campaign will focus on promoted tweets, selected by Twitter. A monthly budget of £15,000 is thought to be able to generate £1 million in sales – this would exceed the additional £800k pcm target. It's based on an average basket of £60, but as we haven't done this before, it could be much lower, so our numbers are based on a lower than average basket of £35.

Media	Budget £	Esti-mated cost per click	Click-through rate %	Poten-tial reach	Click-throughs	Average basket £	Sales Gen-erated £
Twitter	15,000	0.85	3	588235	17647	35	617647

5.2 Systems e.g. Content Marketing

Content Marketing is a major component of many organisations' strategy. It can be a source of differentiation. It can give them an edge. It can attract visitors, help to nurture them into customers and help to retain them.

Content Marketing is all about creating and distributing, at the right time, really relevant content (videos, instagrams, power point slides, tweets, posts, articles, white papers, books and even games) that helps prospects and customers to achieve their goals (e.g. skills improvement or being informed or entertained). Your choice of content ('content strategy') is influenced by your mission, your brand values and brand personality and also what your customers want or would value, that your competitors don't currently share with your stakeholders.

You have to think like a publisher, discover hot topics that are not well served by competitors, brain storm, create content concepts, select the best ones, produce them, distribute them and measure their impact. See the range of content in the content pyramid in 'How Integrated Content Marketing Creates Competitive Advantage (Smith 2014).

You need a team that looks like an egg timer (large at the start, thin in the middle and large at the end . A cross-functional group at the beginning (for brain storming), then a small editorial team and small production team to produce the content, andfinally a large team mobilised to help the distribution (and engagement) at the end. Why not ask your partners, resellers and suppliers to spread your content? GaggleAmp alerts these groups every time you post, makes it easy for them to share and rewards them for sharing. It also integrates with marketing automation systems. Costs $100 pcm if you regularly post content (or less if you are infrequent).

Leverage other content too

Your marketing and advertising team probably have a lot of material that they can share on Instagram. Sharing advertising collateral and any marketing content (PR photos with an added caption) in an organic way simply gets you 'more bang for your buck'. It's inevitable. You leverage, across many tactical channels, the assets you invested in and created (rather than leave them gathering dust). Sift through your assets and then polish and release them in an organised process (or schedule).

See Kelly HR for a full case study of how a team of two generated content that went global and connected with a very specific universe of HR Directors globally.

See Kelly HR for a full case study

Content Wars

Customers are drowning in a sea of content.
Competitors are churning out content – some good
and some bad. Customers' ability to consume
content is finite because there are only so many
hours in a day to read/watch/listen even to really
interesting content.

Mark Schaefer (2014) describes this as the 'Content
Shock' when 'At some point, the amount I am
"paying out" will exceed the amount I am bringing in
and at that point, creating content will not be a smart
business decision for me and many other
businesses.

We may have to pay customers to read our content!
In fact we already are (indirectly as we spend, say 6
hours writing a blog post at a nominal cost of £100
per hour = £600 spent producing the piece!).'

Customers drowning in a sea of content

Content marketing should be designed so that it is easy to measure its impact (is it driving traffic, or is it boosting registrations or sales?) It also must have feedback mechanisms beyond KPIs and analytics, which allow customers to give direct feedback. Build 'Content Pathways' so that when prospects or customers show interest in (open) a particular piece of content, they automatically get sent another, even more relevant, piece of content (or a link to a piece of content).

Content marketing can be a major component in your strategy. But in a hyper-competitive environment you need to have processes in place to monitor which kind of content works best. See the interview regarding 'content marketing and analytics' in the Control section for more.

Meanwhile the highly successful Obama campaign worked hard creatively tocontinually find engaging content for their followers. This simple photograph generated a very high level of engagement. The caption was 'This seat is taken'.

Time spent thinking creatively helped to generate this highly engaging photo during the hugely successful Obama campaign. Photo: Courtesy of Teddy Goff.

5.3 Systems e.g. Marketing Automation System

Once upon a time a sales person could watch a buyer's body language to see what really interested the buyer and whether they were ready to buy.
Today sales people rarely see buyers face-to-face as buyers do a lot of their buying online. Marketers can however, see each potential buyer's digital body language which identifies at what stage in the buying process the visitor is and whether they are ready to buy.
Your click behaviour leaves a trail of your interests, what engaged you, what didn't, and more.

Digital body language
Marketing automation analyses each visitors' digital body language (their click behaviour) and gives each

visitor a particular score which is determined by how interested they are in which products/services.

For example someone who bounces off the first page (exits) might get a minus score; someone who stays 5 minutes looking at product pages gets a higher score, and someone else who looks at product pages, leaves the site and later comes back and watches the product video and moves to the shopping basket (but doesn't buy) gets an even higher score.

These scores and rules allow the system to automatically respond with tailored relevant messages offering more information or help required via the visitors' preferred channel whether a dynamic web page, a pop-up message, an email, a text or even a request to a rep to phone the prospect.

Marketing automation systems help organisations automatically engage with their prospects and customers at the right time, with the right content, via the right channel.

A simple sample marketing automation system

Step 1: Email an invitation to download a free report.
Step 2: Send a thank you to the people who visited the site and downloaded the report.
Step 3: Send them a case study from their industry.
Step 4: If prospect clicks on the case study, create an auto alert for the sales rep to follow up.

The steps required to set up a Marketing Automation programme

1. Clearly define the stages of a sale (and after sale) e.g. visitor/prospect - lead - enquiry - customer - advocate.

2. Define and score digital behaviour required for each stage of a sale e.g. Opening a particular email; Visiting a particular page(s); Downloading a white paper.

3. Clarify what behaviour/score triggers what response.

4. Agree next auto steps for customers that respond ('responders' and 'non responders').

Once this detailed process is rigorously completed an MA programme can:
- integrate social media, direct mail/email, telemarketing and more
- continually serve tailored and highly relevant web landing pages to different visitors
- continually respond via dynamic web pages, dynamic emails, pop up messages
- alert sales or customer service people to call customers

All this without needing assistance from the IT team. You can also set up A/B tests as part of this process to see which pages/offers/photos convert better. The original book on digital body language was written by Steven Woods (co-founder of Eloqua) back in 2009.

5.4 Processes e.g. RFM Database Analysis

Which customers on your database are more likely to keep buying from you? Which customers are worth spending more time and money on (more communications and more rewards)? As mentioned in the Situation Analysis section, database marketers have, for many decades now, used RFM (Recency, Frequency, Monetary) to identify those active customers that are more likely to continue buying throughout their customer lifetime. The ones you might want to invest in - these 'ideal customers'.

Recent customers are more likely to have more active relationships than those who haven't purchased for several years. Equally, more frequent purchasers are more likely to continue purchasing. Monetary means size of purchase - on average bigger spenders are more likely to buy again than small spenders. Latency is often added. Latency means the average duration between purchases. Customers with shorter latency are more likely to purchase again. Many organisations combine RFM to score customers in order to identify which segments of customers are more likely to respond positively.

Here's how it can be used: take 'Recency'. Calculate the average 'recency of purchase' for your customers. Then create two groups: (1) 'More Recent Than Average' - those customers with average frequency and also those with 'more recent' than average frequency. (2) 'Less Recent Than Average' - those customers whose last visit or purchase is less recent than average. Group 2 ('Less

Recent') is most likely to be in the process of defecting (or have already defected). Group 1 ('More Recent') can have a 3-10 times higher response rate. So invest in these.

	More Recent	Less Recent
Customer Source:		
Search Engines	70% of visitors	30% of visitors
Emails	30% of visitors	70% of visitors

Say customers generated by search engines and customers generated by email deliver the same current value. Each dollar spent on either channel is equally profitable. It is also worth checking the potential value of each type of customer, e.g.the potential lifetime value of search visitors might be much higher than visitors generated via email.

Current value and potential value
It is possible to segment your customers using many variables including media used to acquire a customer; keyword phrase used to find the site; content areas visited. It often takes more than one visit to a site before a visitor converts and buys.

The 'How' section explores how we can analyse customer journeys to identify which channels are worth investing more resources in. See Novo, J. - WebTrends Take 10 Series Increase Customer Retention by Analyzing Visitor Segments,

Predicting your customers' future needs

In addition to RFM, purchases can be anticipated by 'time triggers', e.g. six months after a car is bought it needs its first service. 'Date triggered' purchases means a particular date like a birthday or a seasonal event like Father's Day or Christmas Day triggers purchasing of all sorts of products and services. 'Purchase triggered' purchases occur when buying one product suggests the need for a supporting product/service, e.g. when you buy a car you also might want to buy a warranty and certainly, insurance.

Basketball's low hanging fruit

Database Analysis Identifies Best Targets – most likely, least likely and fence sitters.

Professional basketball clubs such as Orlando Magic now analyse their season ticket holders by exploring historic purchasing data and renewal patterns to 'build decision tree models that bucket subscribers into three categories: most likely to renew, least likely and fence sitters.

The fence sitters then get the customer service department's attention come renewal time.'

5.5 Guidelines - social media guidelines

Social Media Guidelines can include attitude, tone, topics, content type, confrontation (how to avoid it) and frequency. Follow the 4-1-1 Rule from Tippingpoint Labs and Joe Pulizzi of the Content Marketing Institute which states, 'For every one self-serving tweet, you should retweet one relevant tweet and most importantly, share four pieces of relevant content written by others.'

Guidelines will include etiquette online – what you can and cannot say. No foul language. No abusive comments. No trade secrets nor sensitive information revealed.

In fact, many guides suggest you should stay positive, despite what comments are thrown at you. Some other guides specify that you must not criticise competition directly. Some guides include key messages, key phrases and/or social media details. Many organisations issue guidelines before a new campaign or initiative starts.

Brand personality and values should be included although a full Brand Guidelines can run into 100 pages, so it is best just to list the key brand guidelines such as personality and values.

Here is The 10-Point Social Media Policy Everyone Will Understand written by Jeff Roach (2014) after a client asked him, the tenth person this year, if he could help them draft a social media policy for their company.

1	Be kind.	
2	You are a person first, an employee second.	
3	Spend most of your time listening and liking (and helping), not posting.	

4	Expectations for professional conduct are the same online as offline (do not criticise a competitor, use foul language etc.).	
5	Do not embarrass or disparage the company.	
6	Do not share private or confidential information (e.g. trade secrets).	
7	Understand your privacy settings but know that any post can accidentally become public.	
8	Pay attention to and support your colleagues' posts.	
9	Be mindful of the reputation you are creating.	
10	Be yourself.	

'Sell something, get a customer.
Help someone, get a customer for life.'
(Jay Baer, 2013)

Here are another ten checklist items covering some of the management aspects of social media

| 11 | Clarify the organisation's social media objectives. | |

12	Clarify the customer experience you want your audiences to enjoy.	
13	Clarify any staff responsibilities whether: (a) optional (e.g. tweet about the company's sales promotions) or	
14	(b) compulsory (e.g. add social media addresses to all email signatures in a consistent style).	
15	Clarify what identify security measures: (a) who has access to which platforms or	
16	(b) how passwords are stored and updated.	
17	Announce where social media integrates: (a) with other company policies (e.g. HR, PR, etc.)	
18	(b) other company marketing communications tools (e.g. ad campaigns, news releases).	
19	Build in crisis planning for senior management: explain how social media can help and hinder during a crisis and also train staff to deliver social media.	
20	Always check your social advice checklists with your legal team.	

Guidelines: 6 tips to exploit the visual opportunity (the shift to visual media)

1	Don't tell if you can show	
2	Create Original Visual Content	
3	Showcase your story: images = emotion and connection	
4	Crowd Source Visual Content: engage fans to create and share images for you; connect and promote your brand visually; contribute to photo and video competition, events	
5	Add back the words: add captions, descriptions ; overlay with call to action; add keywords and hashtags to image descriptions; include watermark or website url on original images	
6	Mix it up: overlay text on instagrams; tweet images and pinterest pins on Twitter; pin videos to pinterest; Use more images on Facbook; include quality images on blog posts	

Source: Dalton (2012) How brands can leverage the power of visual social media, Media Matters, 20 Dec.

5.6 *Checklists* – social media checklist
e.g. LinkedIn

I believe checklists help knowledge transfer and ensure skills are shared around an organisation. It's also good contingency planning (what if a key person leaves, or is ill?) Furthermore, it is good continuity planning.

Here's a very simple five point checklist for using LinkedIn from Jason Miller (2013) This can, and should be, developed into a much more detailed checklist. However it is a good starting point.

		Done: Yes/No
1	Optimize Your LinkedIn Page	
2	Engage Your Audience	
3	Attract More Followers	
4	Follow the 4-1-1 Rule (see the previous social media guidelines)	
5	Analyze	

LinkedIn Social Media Checklist

Better Understanding Of Needs = Better Content
Instead of offering British exporters a newsletter packed with general export advice and a range of case studies, UK Trade and Investment now offer businesses interested in China a newsletter about exporting to China, and a separate newsletter about

exporting to Russia for businesses interested in Russia. UKTI now get much higher open rates and readers rate it more highly. Less is more.

5.7 Constant small improvements

Develop a constant beta culture. Surround yourself with people who become interested in seeing how small changes can make small improvements. 0.5% improvement here and 0.5% improvement there, soon adds up. Constantly split testing ads, emails and landing pages to see if particular phrases, words, images or colours make a difference. This is so important, I'm going to repeat it in the final Control section.

People will become fascinated when they can see, almost immediately, how a change that they make affects the online results. This constant beta culture becomes infectious and nurtures the inquisitive mind: 'What if we tried this...?' as everything can be easily tested. Remember the results do not lie so no more subjective arguments, sit back and watch the results come in. The actual changes in traffic, conversions and repeat buys will appear for all to see. Here's an example of how simplifying a form (reducing 'form friction') boosted sales by 2000%.

Simplifying HSBC sign-up form
HSBC's old registration page had become a barrier by asking too many questions (too early in the relationship) and demanding too much of the new currencies (privacy and time). The form below, with its 17 fields of data, generated just two enquiries per

week. The long list of questions irritates visitors and creates 'form friction' ie the registration form becomes a barrier.

Old enquiry form (17 fields of data) generated two enquiries per week.

Make an Appointment

We'll be in touch to arrange a date and time convenient for you.

I prefer to be contacted by:

○ Phone   ○ Email

Name:

[   ]

Email Address:

[   ]

Contact Number :

[   ] Go

The proposed new form with just 3 fields met with initial internal resistance to this simplification programme which was based on two factors:

1. It would encourage frivolous and sometimes idiotic enquiries from the likes of Donald Duck and Arnold Schwarzenegger.

2. The old form (with 17 fields) gathered data that integrated well into the existing internal system, i.e. it worked and 'if it ain't broke why fix it?'

Yes the old form (requiring answers to 17 fields) did work or function properly but it also created a major psychological barrier. It drove potential customers away. Most visitors did not have time, nor the inclination to share this amount of personal data at this stage in the buying process. Not surprisingly, the old form did not generate sufficient enquiries for a business the size of HSBC. After much discussion it was finally agreed to radically change the form and reduce the number of fields from 17 to just 4: Name, eMail, Phone Number and contact preference.
Result: New enquiry form generated 180 enquiries

per week, boosting revenues from $1m to £20m per quarter (McGovern, 2010).

Small changes can reap big results. But also small changes can deliver smaller improvements which also really have an impact on the bottom line. 6 months of continually finding 0.5% improvement will have a significant impact on your profits. Nurture this culture – the constant beta culture.

5.7 Internal marketing

Some call this Internal Marketing – spending time and money communicating your plans to your internal teams and inspiring them to get behind your plans. Some companies spend 10% of their marketing budget ensuring their staff understand, believe in and become capable of delivering your new plans.

Remember I said that many, if not most, companies are dysfunctional and siloed to a greater or lesser degree. Remember I also said that most staff have a neurotic resistance to new ideas. Incidentally, this is partly why 50% of the world's largest CRM (Customer Relationship Management) projects fail.

Communicating, training and motivating your staff is the key to great execution. Are all of your staff fully behind your social media efforts? Will they seed your marketing content where appropriate (will they send some of your content to the influencers in their own networks)? Do your staff really believe in your product or service? Do you make them feel proud of it? Do they feel proud of it? Here's the acid test: How many of your staff are brand advocates?

Will these staff advocates deliver the very best execution? Would they be as motivated as this staff advocate who made, arguably, the ultimate shockvertisement for his company? Do not try this at home! Beware, you may find this revolting.

This man is sufficiently motivated that he made his own 'Shockvertising' video for his company . See it on www.prsmith.org/blog. Will this start a surge of employee product demo ads?

Also remember, even if they are motivated, they have to have the right skills across a range of new marketing roles in an ever-changing marketing team.

A newly-structured marketing department might look like this:

Campaign Manager The campaign manager plans and executes an automated marketing campaign based on buyer behavior and customer readiness.

Content Strategist Your content represents the voice of your company. Demand generation begins with knowing your audience and buyer personas.

Designer The shift towards visual means you need eye-catching imagery, videos, books, and site layouts that attract and guide visitors easily through your site.

Developer To develop web apps, interaction, smart content and marketing automation programmes that filter relevant messages and content.

Systems Administrator To integrate marketing automation, CRM, social and financials while securing the integrity of customer data.

Analyst Measuring marketing performance and gaining marketing insights that improve marketing decisions, i.e. boost returns.

Adapted from Doyle Slayton (2014) 6 Talents of Modern Day Marketers, LinkedIn 13 May

---

Is 'Action' (execution) more important than Strategy?

A professor once said: 'An "A" execution of a "C" strategy will beat a "C" execution of an "A" strategy

---

every time.' However, I believe that a lousy strategy like the Sinclair C5 eCar strategy, kills a product no matter how excellent the execution. NB the C5 execution was good as it delivered national press coverage (massive awareness) and national distribution on every high street (fantastic distribution). But it failed because of a fundamentally flawed strategy, despite great execution.

Now let's add the final section of your plan, the Control section. This means metrics. Who needs to see what metrics when and, most importantly, what do you do if the metrics are up or down significantly. How oftern do you measure what, how much does it cost, how long does it take etc.

Chapter 6

Control

6.1 Building 'control' into your plan

Your plan needs to include control systems that let you know whether you are on target to achieve the objectives you set earlier. You don't want to wait until the end of the year, when it's too late, to change your tactics. You need early warning systems.

The 'Control' section of your plan lists which KPIs are measured daily and which are measured monthly or quarterly. This section of your plan also specifies who measures what, when and how much it costs. This puts you in control.

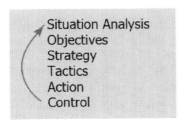

All the metrics you measure at the end of the year will be used in next year's Situation Analysis when analysing performance (results).

The 'Performance/results section in the Situation Analysis is used to set realistic Objectives. The objectives then need to be controlled, or monitored regularly.

You can see the cyclical nature of Objectives – Control – Situation Analysis.

Your plan should specify what will be measured, by
whom, when (how frequently), and most importantly,
what happens if you are way below or above the
target? Your plan may include guidelines about
which manager should be alerted if something is not
working and also if something is working really well.

Here are the objectives we looked at in the
Objectives section. The actual performance is
monitored and fed into various types of reporting
systems (or dashboards).

6.2 Measuring the KPIs

KPI	Results Previous Period	Objective Current Period	Results Current Period
ROI (Return On Investment)			
Sales - units - value			
Market Share - units - value			
Market Leader Number (in top 5)			
Awareness Level (offline survey)			

Measuring KPIs (contd.)

Preference Level (offline survey)			
NPS Score (Net Promoter Score)			
Sentiment Score (incl. competitor comparison)			

Website/Blog
  Unique Visitors
  Average Duration
  Subscribers to
updates/Newsletter
  Leads generated			

Cost Per Visitor (website)			
Cost Per Like (Facbook)			
Cost Per Lead			
Cost Per Customer Acquisition			
Cost Per Customer Retention			
Database Size			
Prospects/Leads			
Customers			
Advocates			
Influencers			

Measuring Web Site KPIs

KPI			
Site Visits	Results Previous Period	Object-ive Current Period	Results Current Period
Unique Visitors			
Bounce Rate			
Duration			
Page Views passive engagement			
Most Popular Page(s)			
Most popular downloads			
Engagement - Downloads			
Engagement - Likes/Favourites			
Engagement - Comments			
Engagement - Shares			
Engagement - Registrations/Newsletter			
Churn Rate			
Conversions - Leads & Sales			
Sales (all sales)			
Task Completion			
SCAR (Shopping Cart Abandonment Rate)			

Satisfaction Score			
NPS Score			
Sentiment Score			
Share of Voice			

Social Media Platforms – repeat for each platform			
Followers/Likes – engagement etc.			

'We prefer the discipline of knowledge
to the anarchy of ignorance.
We pursue knowledge the way a pig pursues truffles

David Ogilvy, Ogilvy & Mather, Corporate Culture,
What we believe and how we behave: Nine Obiter Dicta

You may find it helpful to use the sales funnel to monitor firstly, the number of visitors and secondly, the number converting to an opportunity (filling in a form, or watching a product demonstration/becoming a hotter prospect or lead), followed by the number converting to sales).

The Sales Funnel

The funnel can be further analysed so we can see the actual cost per visitor, cost per lead and cost per order. There are many different formats for dashboards. The dashboard on the next page is from www.Smart-Insights.com.

The columns across the top show where traffic is coming from: Advertising (ad network), Search (paid search & natural search), Partners (affiliates, aggregators, sponsorship, email).

Costs and revenues are in the left hand side column: Media Costs (set up/creative, CPM, CPC, Media Costs, Total Costs); Media Impressions & Response (impressions, Click Through Rate, site visits); Conversion To Opportunity/Lead (number of opportunities, cost per opportunity); Conversion to Sales (sales, % of sales & Cost Per Sale); Costs & Profitability are also tracked across every channel.

		Advertising		Search		Partners				All digital media channels
Home		Ad buys (CPM)	Ad network (CPM)	Paid search (CPC)	Natural search	Affiliates (CPA)	Aggregators (CPA)	Sponsorship (Fixed)	Email list (CPM)	Total or Average
	Setup/ creative / Mgt costs	£0	£0	£0	£0	£0	£0	£0	£0	£0
	CPM	£10.0	£10.0	£4.0	£1.8	£10.0	£20.0	£100.0	£10.0	£4.3
Media costs	CPC	£5.0	£5.0	£0.20	£0.90	£5.0	£10.0	£33.3	£100.0	£0.6
	Media costs	£10,000	£10,000	£30,000	£30,000	£10,000	£10,000	£10,000	£10,000	£120,000
	Total cost setup & media	£10,000	£10,000	£30,000	£30,000	£10,000	£10,000	£10,000	£10,000	£120,000
	Budget %	8%	8%	25%	25%	8%	8%	8%	8%	120%
Media impressions	Impressions or names	1,000,000	1,000,000	7,500,000	16,666,667	1,000,000	500,000	100,000	10,000	27,776,667
&	CTR	0.2%	0.2%	2.0%	0.2%	0.2%	0.2%	0.3%	1.0%	0.7%
Response	Clicks or site visits	2,000	2,000	150,000	33,333	2,000	1,000	300	100	190,733
Conversion	Conversion rate to opportunity	100.0%	100.0%	100.0%	100.0%	100.0%	100.0%	100.0%	100.0%	100.0%
to	Number of opportunities	2,000	2,000	150,000	33,333	2,000	1,000	300	100	190,733
Opportunity (Lead)	Cost per opportunity	£5.0	£5.0	£0.2	£0.9	£5.0	£10.0	£33.3	£100.0	£0.6
Conversion	Conversion rate to sale	100.0%	100.0%	100.0%	100.0%	50.0%	100.0%	100.0%	100.0%	93.6%
to	Number of sales	2,000	2,000	150,000	33,333	1,000	1,000	300	100	189,733
Sales	% of sales	1.1%	1.1%	79.1%	17.6%	0.5%	0.5%	0.2%	0.1%	100.0%
	Cost per sale (CPA)	£5.0	£5.0	£0.2	£0.9	£10.0	£10.0	£33.3	£100.0	£0.6
Revenue	Total revenue	£100,000	£100,000	£7,500,000	£1,666,667	£50,000	£50,000	£15,000	£5,000	£9,486,667
		£70,000	£70,000	£5,250,000	£1,166,667	£35,000	£35,000	£10,500	£3,500	£6,640,667
Costs		£10,000	£10,000	£30,000	£30,000	£10,000	£10,000	£10,000	£10,000	£120,000
		£80,000	£80,000	£5,280,000	£1,196,667	£45,000	£45,000	£20,500	£13,500	£6,760,667
Profitability	Profit	£20,000	£20,000	£2,220,000	£470,000	£5,000	£5,000	-£5,500	-£8,500	£2,726,000
	Return on investment	25.0%	25.0%	42.0%	39.3%	11.1%	11.1%	-26.8%	-63.0%	40.3%

Online Media Mix model - based on % budget - with example of 'average' CTR

This dashboard is from www.SmartInsights.com. The columns and rows are explained on the previous page. Apologies for the tiny print. You can, download your own spreadsheets and templates from Smart Insights (you must register on the site).

Note:
1. CPM and CPC calculated based on total cost for comparison
2. This is not a full ROI or lifetime value model since future lifetime value not included
3. For SEO, budget is automatically placed into setup/creative costs and you have to estimate the number of clicks this will deliver
4. For affiliate marketing, work back from Cost per sale to calculate sales, opportunities and clicks, so changing click-through and conversion rates impacts cells to the left rather than right.
5. The blue cells indicate the main control parameters for each media which are important to improving cost effectiveness.

How to use this spreadsheet
1. First define expected conversion rates to opportunity (lead) and sale for different media (can be set to same value for simplicity).
2. Then establish realistic costs for purchasing different media (CPM, CPA, CPC) as appropriate for your market.
3. Finally vary the mix of impressions for different media, remembering that there are limits to media that can be purchased (e.g. number of search terms). Vary the impressions to maximise the number of sales and minimise CPA while also minimising the risk of purchasing too much of one type of media - a more balanced budget diversifies risk.
4. To compare the effectiveness of media look at differences in media for CPS and as a percentage of budget and as a percentage of sales.

DISCLAIMER
This spreadsheet is provided in good faith for modelling budgets and performance for digital marketing. Smart Insights (Marketing Intelligence) Limited cannot be held responsible for the consequences of any errors in, or misinterpretation of, the spreadsheet models or for any actions taken as a result of using this spreadsheet. Please ask questions or let me know if you believe there are formula errors, so that we can update.

The illusion that communication has taken place

'The single biggest problem in communication is the illusion that it has taken place.'
George Bernard Shaw.
Yes this is often the case, but we now have tools to actually check and see if communications are working and how comms affects awareness and behaviour. PR Smith

---

Using spread sheets and funnels helps you to be in control, see what's working (and then increase this) and see what's not working (modify it, test it or decrease it).

But beware of being overwhelmed by information and analytics. Information fatigue syndrome is causing people to become ill as they struggle to manage all the information thrown at them. So be focused about what key information you really need to make better decisions.

Too much info and not enough action
'What data is valuable and what data isn't?
Stop wasting time on stuff that doesn't help you.'
Steve Jackson (2011) Cult of Analytics

So in addition to regularly monitoring dashboards stuffed with metrics, you also need to schedule the following control mechanisms into your plan:

- Website Usability Testing
- Website Satisfaction Monitoring
- Website NPS
- Website Bounce Rate
- Website Traffic Quality
- Which Channels Deliver Best Quality Visitors
- Social Media Supporting The Brand Delivering Results
- Content Marketing Supporting The Brand Delivering Results
- Share Of Voice – is it too small?

6.2 Is your website under control?

Does Your Website Work Properly?

Or does it enrage your visitors with dead ends, broken links, error 404s, shopping carts that crash and worse? London 2012 was a great Olympics but buying tickets on the website proved too difficult for many. The Glasgow 2014 Commonwealth Games website ticket malfunction resulted in headlines like:

Web site fiasco
Sale of Commonwealth Games tickets suspended in website fiasco The Guardian 14 May 2014

How could this happen again? What kind of web usability testing did they carry out? Rugby World Cup 2015 hosted in England has made improvements. But how can the other ticket fiascos be allowed to happen?

Usability testing

Usability Testing asks various stakeholders to carry out specific tasks whilst being observed, e.g. a journalist is asked to find last month's press release or blog update; an investor is asked to find the annual report; a customer is asked to find product x and buy it etc. This usually identifies any glaring problems with the website. It's basic stuff but how come the Olympics 2012 , Glasgow 2014 and Rugby World Cup websites did not function fully when tickets went on sale? Schedule usability testing into your plan.

Does your website satisfy your visitors?

You can do a separate 'pop up' survey just as a visitor is leaving your site. Remember to check that the people answering the survey are in your target market group. An exit pop up survey must be short and should be limited to just a handful of questions.

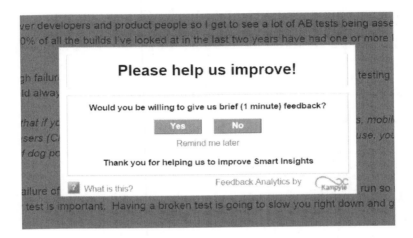

Does your website generate a positive nps score?

Or even a one question pop up; 'On a scale of 1-10, how likely are you to recommend this site to someone else? 1 being 'never' and 10 being 'definitely'. This is at the heart of Net Promoter Score (NPS) where you count all the 1-6 scores as negatives and all the 9-10 scores as positive. Ignore 7-8. Then take negative score from positive score to get NPS.

Is 88% bounce rate and 1% conversion good or bad?

A bounce rate of 88% and a conversion rate of 1% - is this good or bad?

A bounce rate of 88% means approximately 9/10 visitors don't find your site relevant/interesting and leave it after only visiting one page.

A conversion rate of 1% means that only 1 in 100 sign up or convert. Either we need to improve the site or we are getting the wrong traffic. Find the industry average conversion rate (from Google Analytics benchmarking: Hitwise data). If it's 3% then yes, this is an issue that needs fixing immediately.

Is 96% scar (shopping cart abandonment rate) good or bad?

Bad if 50% is the average SCAR from across your industry. Good, or at least, marginally better if 99% is the norm across your industry for the last 6 months! What actions do you take? Expert walk through Shopping Cart experience? Do an exit survey to find out why?

To improve SCAR requires resources. To get resources you need to tell management about losing £250k pw from SCAR rather than talking about reducing shopping cart abandonment from 96% to 50%.

Remember customers abandoning shopping carts also get annoyed and some of them get angry and vociferous. So it really is worth analysing and fixing a high abandonment rate.

Some customers get angry. Although you can't see them online you can still monitor them (and respond to them online).

Is your traffic under control? - the right visitors - VQVC

Given that there are so many metrics, you might find VQVC a useful reminder of four measures that are worth analysing: Volume, Quality, Value and Cost. Volume typically measures traffic (unique visitors, visits, page views etc.). Quality measures the quality of the type of visitor (measured by bounce rate, duration, pages per visit). Value measures ultimately £ sales value which a particular campaign might generate by driving a visitor to visit/like/download or even buy when visiting a particular page.

This involves assigning £ value to click behaviour, e.g. Nokia estimated the value of a non-Facbook fan customer was only worth $63 compared to Facbook fan customers at $171; Coca Cola $120 v $190; Red bull $50 v $113; Nike $83 v $205 (Chaffey & Smith, 2013).

Finally, Costs means calculating the Cost per Acquisition (of a visitor; of a lead; of a sale). For more see 'How to make the most of Google Analytics', Smart Insights, 2014.

Are your channels under control - multichannel funnels – analytics

Go back to Situation Analysis, Customer Analysis, 'How do customers buy?' I mentioned Google's Multichannel funnel analysis tools to monitor their online journey, e.g. 'How long do your visitors take to make a purchase? How many channels do your visitors use? etc., since customers generally make more than one visit to a site before buying.

Their multiple visits also often come from many different channels whether a general organic search (via a search engine) or a branded search, a PPC Ad, a link, or by directly inserting the web address into a browser.

Multichannel funnels give marketers more control as they can see which channels are assisting the sales and what the preferred journeys (or combination of channels) are.

This puts marketers in control of their destiny as they can now make informed decisions about where is the optimum channel to spend their resources.

Multi-Channel Funnels Report video is on Youtube

Is your social media under control and always enhancing your brand?

Although we'll dedicate the final section of SOSTAC® to 'control', it is worth mentioning now that without social media guidelines (and for that matter, PR Guidelines) major faux pas (mistakes) occur.

Senior management normally avoid any undesirable press coverage.

Today, as social media makes everyone a 'citizen journalist' a casual comment picked up by someone with a mobile phone can be a source of constant embarrassment.

As Ged Carroll says, 'There is no longer any off the record.' And I'm not talking about QPR's premiere league fullback, Rio Ferdinand's irresponsible tweets that brought the game into disrepute, invoked a large fine and a three match suspension. I'm talking about the chairman of VW making comments about competition within the range of video cameras.

At the Frankfurt Motor Show in 2011 Volkswagen Chairman Martin Winterkorn was filmed admiring the Hyundai i30 model. In particular, he noticed the lack of noise on the adjustable steering wheel.

As he spoke to his chief designer, his embarrassing comments were recorded to create a video much cited by his South Korean rivals.

VW chairman caught on camera on Youtube commenting on competition at the 2011 Frankfurt Motor Show

"Why can they do it? BMW cannot do it, we cannot do it" said the unguarded VW chairman. (Foy, 2014). Almost 2m people have watched this video on youtube alone.
Training your staff and issuing social media guidelines not only reduces the risk of major faux pas, but it also helps when you want to spread your marketing content and announcements since your staff can help to seed your content into their own networks (if the staff deem it appropriate).

6.3 Is your marketing content under control?

Whether you are producing a book, book, video, instagrams, blog posts, tweets (remember the content pyramid in the action section), you need to think about controlling content metric goals.

This means that equipped with a clearly defined audience and clearly defined goals, you brain storm, select and produce content.

If the goal is to generate conversions to newsletter registration and eventually conversion to revenue, then make sure your content has a direct way to make this happen, i.e. add direct links to these landing pages so it becomes easy to measure the effectiveness of your content.

Watch this 25 minute video about 'How To Measure The Effectiveness Of Content Marketing' (courtesy of Steve Farnsworth and Erin Robbins), on www.PRSmith.org/blog. It really puts marketing content and analytics together very nicely.

Erin Robbins
on the Effectiveness Of Content Marketing

6.4 Is your share of voice under control?

In this case, 'Share of Voice' is the percentage of all online content and conversations about your company, or your brand, compared to your competitors. Do you have a presence in important conversations? What about competition?

Then you start asking if you should increase or reduce your presence? Are people making positive or negative comments about your company or brand? How quickly do you respond (if at all)? Do the responses satisfy those making the comments? If you don't know or can't see what your target market is saying about you on a quantitative, qualitative, and tonal basis then you are 'marketing in the dark with a blindfold on' (Cramer, 2014). It is simply essential to see what is being said about you. There is no choice here.

Word-of-mouth brings us back to the old PR days when agencies would gather the newspapers and magazines (and check TV and radio) and count how many mentions the brand got (compared to the competition) and later they scored them either positive or negative according to good and bad mentions. After that came a single score.

Today we call it sentiment analysis. Since all media has fragmented into smaller, better-targeted media including blogs, Facbook and Twitter streams, then there are a lot more people publishing their 'voice'. You also need to listen to what is being said about your competitors (and your own business). Hence Sentiment Analysis has become popular – with some boards of directors wanting to see the sentiment score reported regularly.

As well as Search Engine Share Of Voice, there is also Advertising Share Of Voice (Meinertzhagen, 2013). You can see more in appendix 8.

Turn information into action.
Use information to make better decisions.
Ask yourself 'what information do I need to make a great decision?'
PR Smith

6.5 Developing a constant beta culture

Without a constant beta culture or a constant A/B testing culture you are playing pot luck, as opposed to constantly optimising your emails, ads, landing pages etc. so that your results continually improve.

You'll find you can do more for less and the money saved can be spent somewhere else where, perhaps, you desperately need more budget. However, be thorough with your A/B testing.

'It simply means that if you *aren't* checking your AB tests work in all the devices (tablets, mobile, desktop, laptop) *and* browsers (Chrome, Internet Explorer, Firefox, Safari) that your customers use, your test is probably a pile of dog poo.' (Sullivan, 2014)

Using real time analytics to make better real time marketing mix decisions

So here's what 1-800-FLOWERS.COM (working with SAS) now do – they quickly spot issues and remedy them. What if a fulfilment florist in a certain ZIP code delivers late or has to substitute inferior flowers?

They can now see complaints and low scores in real time and automatically adjust orders sent to the distributor florist based on consumer concerns.

They also adjust the product mix offered on the Website. If too many florists are struggling to get a certain kind of tulip called for in a particular bouquet (and thus customers complain about substitutions), 1-800-FLOWERS.COM can quickly spot this trend and remove the bouquet from its Website temporarily (if it's just a temporary shortage) or permanently if necessary.

They estimate that this has improved its enterprise customer service value ratio by 100 basis points, which translates to millions in revenue.
Desai, N. Making customer connections bloom, Saas Customer Stories

---

6.6 Constant learnings and insights

In addition to presenting their KPIs at the end of the year Procter & Gamble ask their managers to present up to seven 'learnings' or insights that they've gleaned from their marketplace. Here are two examples from Smart Insights Party case:

(1) Google Analytics (GA) reveals Pinterest impact on sales

GA shows that Pinterest drives an average of 1,000 new sales to our website each month. Whilst this is relatively low, these are higher spending visitors with an average spend of £140. They particularly buy the 'party packs' and 25% of them opt for the express delivery service.

(2) Customer research reveals preference for images v discount stories

Our website includes a space where our visitors can share their purchase with friends. Less than 0.5% do so. Customer research has revealed that this is because customers did not want to admit to 'having spent only £15 on a knockout necklace'. So rather than sharing purchase information, we'll ask customers to share images of the product and/or images wearing the jewellery on the website, Facbook, Twitter and Pinterest. We know that when images are shared, sales are generated.
Clickthrough to sale from an image is 0.5%.
Therefore the more images that are available and the more that the images are shared, the more sales increase.

Your analytics can reveal some real insights about customers. This and all other KPIs can be subsequently used in the next 'Situation Analysis.

Marketers often measure the wrong things
Like satisfaction (product/service satisfaction), engagement, interaction, relationships, loyalty. So much marketing and branding hyperbole.
What are they missing?

We don't always want to engage. We don't always want an experience. Sometimes, we just want to get things done as quickly and easily as possible. Gerry McGovern

So why is usability so often ignored?

'Amazon has known for a long time that the further away they pushed the login process the more they sold. If you make it simpler, people buy more. If you make it simpler, people stay with you longer. Reducing hassle increases sales.'
(Gerry McGovern, 2014). Do we measure this 'reducing hassle'?

Monitoring and measurement can motivate staff
Earnestly monitoring KPIs to identify problems earlier rather than later, so your team
can make changes to ensure they hit their targets. Rewards for achieving KPIs (need to think this through carefully – as people will expect it after a while). Non-financial rewards, e.g. gifts (which are also called 'psychic income' if the gifts appeal to their

higher level needs of being loved, self-esteem and self-realisation) can be much more motivating (and sometimes cost less if you get trade prices or bulk discounts!)

Monitoring and measuring stops wasting money
Having good control systems in place reveals what works well (and therefore do more of this sooner rather ran later) and also shows what isn't working so well.

Good monitoring systems stop money from being wasted and ensures that money spent is constantly optimised.

Good control systems stop money being wasted.

6.7 90 Day Planning

90 day planning can help ensure your plan delivers the right results. A quarterly or 90 day focus helps to break down the annual plan into manageable parts which are then broken down by month and week.

KPI	Jan	Feb	Mar	Q1 Total
Site Visitors	10,000	10,000	10,000	30,000
Leads	1,000	1,000	1,000	1,000
Total Units	100	100	100	300
Total ASP	£10	£10	£10	£10
Total revenue	£1,000	£1,000	£1,000	£3,000

Monitoring KPIs does not always have to involve a lot of manual spreadsheet work; you can use APIs and feeds to automate the preparation of these results tables (e.g. using the Google Analytics API).

90 day plans should include:

- KPIs for the 90 days broken down by month
- Key milestones for tactics (e.g. launch new content – Best Practice Guide)

- Deliverables required to ensure tactics are delivered on time

Launch new Best Practice Guide

Deliverable	Status	Owner	Deadline
Copy Created	Green	Jim	10 Jan
Visuals sources	Green	Ali	20 Jan
Guide produced	Green	Mel	22 Jan
Influencers contacted	Orange	Ali	22 Jan
eMail created	Orange	Jim	25 Jan
News releases created	Red	Phil	31 Jan

Red = Deliverable is not on track and unlikely to be delivered on time
Amber = Risky, identify underlying problems and address them
Green= on track

You can see how the Control and Action sections can overlap. That's absolutely fine because as long as you include all the elements of SOSTAC®, you will have the foundation for a perfect plan whichever particular final format you decide. Don't forget your 3Ms

Summary

So this is SOSTAC®. Don't forget to add in your 3Ms, the 3 key resources: Men and Women, Money (budgets) & Minutes (timescales).

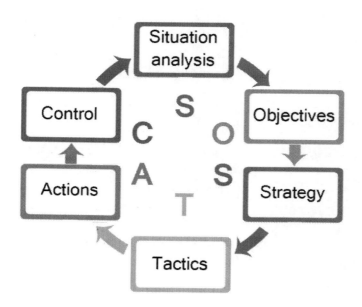

+3Ms – The 3 Key Resources

Men and Women
The human resource. Skilled marketers will be in demand and particularly during this period of radical change to marketing.

Here's another possible marketing team: Digital Marketing Specialist; Social Media Manager; Chief Listening Officer; Content Marketing (including Blogger); SEO Specialist; App Designer; App Developer; Cloud Services Specialist; Big Data Analyst; Market Research Data Miner. If you cannot recruit, train and motivate internally, can you find the people externally in agencies with the right skill sets?

Money
Budgets – you need budgets. Whether 5% of forecasted sales if you are B2C or 1-2% if B2B (up to 8 times higher if it is a new product or service being launched), this percentage of forecasted sales is a common benchmark. However, increasingly marketers will be asked to justify why they need their budgets – reverting to the ideal approach or task approach.

Minutes
Time is often the most limited resource. Particularly when you define what information you need to make a great decision but discover you haven't got the time to collect the information. Add in A/B testing and pilot testing and you'll see why time is at a premium. Incidentally, perhaps it's time to stop thinking about campaigns and start thinking about conversations (and constant beta/constant improvement).

> **Blend Analytics, Engineering and Creativity**
> 'To stay ahead or be a part of this digital upheaval, brands must adopt a hacker mind-set of testing, iterating and improving by blending analytics, engineering and creativity.' (Hudson, 2014).

I hope this SOSTAC® guide has been useful to you, triggered some ideas, helped you to structure your plan or even adopt & integrate it with any other planning structure that you might prefer.

Here are the key points summary inforgraphic of the SOSTAC® system.

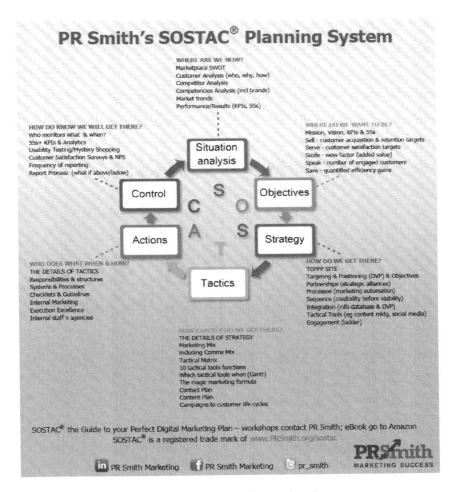

PR Smith's SOSTAC® Planning System

WHERE ARE WE NOW?
Marketplace SWOT
Customer Analysis (who, why, how)
Competitor Analysis
Competencies Analysis (incl brands)
Market trends
Performance/Results (KPIs, SSs)

HOW DO KNOW WE WILL GET THERE?
Who monitors what & when?
SSs+ KPIs & Analytics
Usability Testing/Mystery Shopping
Customer Satisfaction Surveys & NPS
Frequency of reporting
Report Process (what if above/below)

WHERE DO WE WANT TO BE?
Mission, Vision, KPIs & SSs
Sell - customer acquisition & retention targets
Serve - customer satisfaction targets
Sizzle - wow factor (added value)
Speak - number of engaged customers
Save - quantified efficiency gains

Situation analysis

Control

Objectives

S O

C

A S

T

Actions

Strategy

Tactics

WHO DOES WHAT WHEN & HOW?
THE DETAILS OF TACTICS
Responsibilities & structures
Systems & Processes
Checklists & Guidelines
Internal Marketing
Execution Excellence
Internal staff v agencies

HOW DO WE GET THERE?
TOPPP SITE
Targeting & Positioning (OVP) & Objectives
Partnerships (strategic alliances)
Processes (marketing automation)
Sequence (credibility before visibility)
Integration (info database & OVP)
Tactical Tools (eg content mktg, social media)
Engagement (ladder)

HOW EXACTLY DO WE GET THERE?
THE DETAILS OF STRATEGY
Marketing Mix
including Comms Mix
Tactical Matrix
10 tactical tools functions
Which tactical tools when (Gantt)
The magic marketing formula
Contact Plan
Content Plan
Campaigns to customer life cycles

SOSTAC® the Guide to your Perfect Digital Marketing Plan — workshops contact PR Smith; eBook go to Amazon
SOSTAC® is a registered trade mark of www.PRSmith.org/sostac

PRSmith
MARKETING SUCCESS

in PR Smith Marketing   f PR Smith Marketing   pr_smith

Download this &/or the mobile version from
www.PRSmith.org/SOSTAC

Appendices

Appendix 1
Situation Analysis: Analysing Customers
Using Personas
How to develop personas
that boost your conversion rate

Your online business may have three or more customer types, each with different needs/wants/reasons and each with different triggers that motivate a purchase.

---

1. Research and Categorise your customers
– what categories of customers do you have? Demographics (age, gender, relative income,); Needs – what needs are being met?; Ask yourself 'What kind of offers would make this person buy? How do they shop - impulse or deliberate high involvement?' Then ask your customers (and your sales people) the same questions.

---

2. Develop Several Persona or Customer Profiles
Using your research categories, try to narrow down your customer types into, say three groups. Now describe their persona – a brief profile including the demographics, media consumption, social networks, method of buying and key motivators.

---

3. Now take each persona and get right inside their head. Write out in detail (up to two pages). This really helps marketers to write good copy.

---

4. Create a special landing page for each persona.

---

5. Segment visitors into sales paths
Create a step by step walk through covering the complete sales path which this person would like to take.

6. Calls To Action – don't forget them

Copy that is written for the average prospect…
is written for no one in particular and often fails
miserably

Appendix 2
Situation Analysis: Scenario Planning: National Semi Conductor

Like personas, Scenario Planning keeps your copy writers and web designers grounded ground the designers in the world inhabited by the user'. This example is, arguably, the most potent use of scenario planning is it boosted sales and loyalty and created long term sustainable competitive advantage.

This example actually use the customer analysis strategically to develop a UX (User Experience) that engages, satisfies and wows customers. This proves Drucker was right – you are only in business for one reason: 'to help your customers'. Sit back and enjoy this exceptional piece of marketing.

NSC supply analogue and digital microchips that process sounds and images for mobiles and DVDs. Target DMU: Design Engineers and Corporate Purchasing Agents (they don't buy but the choices they make/specify at beginning of NPD determine the components bought later). The website gave information about products.
How can the website help engineers?

Launched a project to **develop a deep understanding of engineers**… including how they work. This helped them learn how they design components. This led them to consider creating online tools (on the website) to help engineers.

Focused on 'power supplies'.
Design engineers under time pressure.
Easy to use tools could speed design process and save time.

Put a multi-functional team together.
Marketing, application designers, web designers, engineers…

Customers work process – identify a design engineer's work process.
1. Create a part 2. Create a design 3. Analyse the design (simulations)
2. Build a prototype

Created an online tool web based tool called 'web-bench'
Engineers complete the whole design process without special software. Engineer logs on – he is prompted to specify overall parameter and key components

Web bench auto-generates possible designs and complete technical specs;
Part lists; prices; and cost benefit analysis.
Engineer then **refines the design**. Runs real time **simulation** (using sophisticated that Nat. Semi had licensed and offers it on its site).

Engineer can then **alter the design** many times.
Save iterations in my portfolio. Email link to **colleagues** so they can run and save simulations.

Once engineer agrees the final design, system generates **a bill of materials for the prototype** c/w Nat Semi's components and all requirements from other manufacturers c/w links to distributors and prices.

Result: Do in 2 hours what previously took months.
Design engineers loved it.
Designed more than **20,000** power supplies in the first year of operation.

What next? Asked engineers about other activities they had difficulty with. Thermal simulations and circuitry … new scenarios for engineers who design wireless devices… **created web therm… end of year 31,000 visitors on site… 3,000 orders or referrals every day.** One integrated socket = **40m units with Nokia. This was 10+ years ago!**

Source: Seybold P (2001) Get Inside the Lives of your customers.   HBR May

Appendix 3
Situation Analysis: Digital Body Language - KPMG visitor types segmented by click behaviour

Web site traffic provides a wealth of information that can, and should be, used in the Situation Analysis as it reveals what stage in the buying process various visitors are and it highlights any visitors who are hot prospects deserving special attention. So here's some additional insights into how KPMG use digital body language (click behaviour) to categorise their visitors.

Type	Description	Identification
Prospect	A visitor who submits an RFP or an email to a partner.	A visit that includes an RFP submission or an email to a partner.
Participant	A visitor who registers for an event, the site or content.	A visit that includes a submission of a registration form.
Passive Browser	A visitor who downloads single articles, papers, starts but doesn't finish a video.	A visit that includes a single page view or download, or video view.
Researcher	A visitor who downloads multiple articles, papers, starts and completes more than one video in multiple practice areas or industries.	A visit that includes downloading multiple articles, papers, video start/complete.

Type	Description	Identification
Advocate	A visitor who reads an article or paper, or views a video and shares it.	A visit that includes content consumption and sharing of that content.
Focused Seeker	A visitor who reads multiple content items within a practice area or industry.	A visit that includes multiple touches of content with a practice area or industry section. This visit segment may be used in conjunction with any of the previous segments.
Passive Job Seeker	A visitor who reads content on the Jobs section of the site.	A visit that includes one view of the site content and then leaves the site.
Engaged Job Seeker	A visitor who submits a job search query and views Job Details.	A visit that includes at least one job search query and view of Job Details page.
Participating Job Seeker	A visitor that submits their résumé.	A visit that includes submission of at least one résumé on a Job Details page.

Type	Description	Identification
Brand Aware Visitor – First Time and Repeat	A visitor that comes to the site directly.	A visit that begins through a bookmark or direct input of a global or local KPMG URL.
Responder	A visitor who responds to a KPMG email campaign, or clicks on a link within an alert or newsletter.	A visit that originates with a referral from a link to KPMG web content through a KPMG sourced communication.
Brand Aware Searcher	A visitor who comes to KPMG website through branded SEO, PPC, display ads on third party sites.	A visit that originates with a referral from a link to KPMG web content through a search engine, display ad, or other media where KPMG brand is evident.
Non-Brand Aware Searcher	A visitor who comes to KPMG website through non-branded SEO or PPC.	A visit that originates with a referral from a link to KPMG web content through a search engine.
Passive Social Visitor	A visitor that comes from a social media property (Facbook, Twitter, YouTube) one time.	A visit that originates as a referral from a social media property.

Type	Description	Identification
Engaged Social Visitor	A visitor that comes from a social media property (Facbook, Twitter, YouTube) and conducts one of the Engagement actions described in the Metrics Taxonomy.	A visit that originates as a referral from a social media property and ends with the described Engagement task.

KPMG

Appendix 4
Situation Analysis: The UX is different on the mobile

Here's a very nicely written two parts from Goldberg (2013), Marketing on Mobile: Why is this Platform Different?

Part 1: So write content differently.

As more and more people adopt smartphones, B2B content marketers are thinking about how to bring their content to mobile users. It's no wonder. comScore, Inc., a leader in measuring the digital world, reported that 55 percent of mobile users in the U.S., 129.4 million people, owned smartphones during the three months ending in January 2013 — a seven percent increase since October.

But clearly, you can't simply take your existing marketing content and move it to a mobile device. You need to create new content in a format best suited to the strengths and limitations of this medium. In this two-part series on writing content for mobile devices, I'll talk first about why the experience of reading content is different on mobile. In part two, I'll discuss ways to write content to better suit mobile devices.

Why is mobile different?

When you do any type of writing, it's always a good idea to put yourself in the shoes of your reader. The experience of reading on a mobile device is different than reading on a standard desktop, laptop or tablet for three reasons:

- **Constant interruption.** When you're at a computer, people are more likely to assume you're working and leave you alone. If you're looking at a smartphone in a room filled with people, there's a greater chance you'll be interrupted.

- **Multitasking.** There's a much greater chance your reader is multitasking with their smartphone. For example, a dad might be looking up football scores on his smartphone while waiting for his daughter's chorus performance to begin; a manager may check for text messages or emails while waiting online at the Starbucks drive through.

- **Small screen size.** The most significant difference between desktop machines and smartphones is the size of the screen. Looking at a smaller screen is more likely to cause eye strain. More importantly, it's harder to retain information and comprehension is lower on these screens.

Why small screens reduce comprehension

According to research presented in the book "Mobile Usability" by Jakob Nielsen and Raluca Budiu, it's 108% more difficult to understand information when reading from a mobile screen compared to reading on a desktop screen. Comprehension suffers for two reasons:

- **Less visible context.** The less you can see, the more you have to remember when you're trying to understand anything that's not fully explained within the viewable space. Because human short-term memory is notoriously weak, less context translates into lower comprehension.

- **More scrolling.** Mobile users have to scroll around more to see other parts of the content rather than simply glancing at the text. Scrolling takes more time, which degrades memory. It also diverts attention from the problem at hand to locating the appropriate part of the page. Additionally, you need to find your previous place on the page.

In the second part of this series, I'll present ways to write content to address these issues.

What other factors contribute to a mobile screen making content marketing more challenging on a mobile device?

Part 2: How to write content for mobile devices

In part one of this two-part series, I talked about why your marketing content needs to be different on mobile devices. In this second part, I address how to write content that will be effective on these devices.

As I mentioned last time, the experience of reading on mobile devices is different from that of a desktop, laptop, or tablet device for three reasons: mobile users are more likely to be interrupted, they're more likely to be multitasking, and the small screen size means that reading comprehension plummets.

So how do you create content that will have an impact under these circumstances? First, consider the types of content that will be most compelling to smartphone users. You can always ask people what they want. But as a rule of thumb, some types of content that are better suited to mobile include non-editorial content, such as data or an app like a specialty calculator. In terms of written content, start with news content or any content that's constantly updated.

Next, when you write your content, follow these 9 tips:

1. **Less is best.** Use shorter sentences. Get rid of any unnecessary words or images. Avoid long pages that require a lot of scrolling.
2. **Get to the point fast.** State the most useful, relevant information at the start.
3. **Do one thing at a time.** Put only one idea on each page.
4. **State clear goals.** Make clear what action you'd like the reader to take - whether that's sharing your content or signing up for your mailing list.
5. **Make text scannable.** Break up text into small chunks or paragraphs. This will add white space between text, making it easier to read and scan. Bulleted lists will make information even more scannable.
6. **Grab the reader.** Use sensory words, such as feel, savor, scent, that paint a vivid picture in the reader's mind.
7. **Use contractions and abbreviations.**
8. **Summarize.** When presenting longer pieces, create an executive summary of

the content with a link that they can read later on a tablet, laptop or PDF.

9. Think multiple platforms. Make it easy to move content cross-platform. For   example, by adding a prominent "email this" link.
Cheryl Goldber, C (2013) Marketing on Mobile: Why is this Platform Different?High Tech Communicator, 3 June

Appendix 5
Situation Analysis: New Ways To Know Your Customer

How cookies, digital body language, big data and marketing automation help you to know your customer

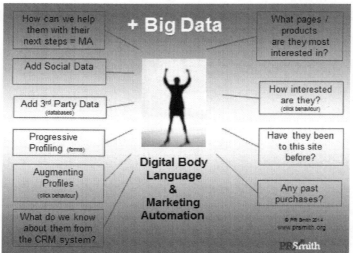

The increasing amount of customer data available

A Cookie

Is a small bit of code which is lodged on a visitor's own browser once they visit a site (after asking the visitor's permission). Visitors can delete cookies anytime. It can contain visitor preferences, language preferences, or display settings, past interactions plus any other information that the website has but more often than not, this data will be held separately in a marketing database with the cookie being a user identification which acts as a key to access the rich data collected about a visitor (or customer). A cookie looks like this: UserID A9A3BECE0563982D

The click behaviour (what they click on) is recorded and tells us what pages they looked at, how long they spent looking at them, and if they've been to the site before. It can also link to the marketing database and can see whether the visitor has bought from us before, plus any issues identified in the CRM system such as 'Salesforce'.

On-Site Behaviour (or click behaviour) is recorded. This tells us what products a customer is interested in (duration plus if they've looked at the product video etc.). Click behaviour is digital body language. It identifies how interested a visitor is, e.g. if they leave ('bounce') after a few seconds they get a very low score. If they stay over, say, 5 minutes, look at a product page, watch a product video, download the product spec and add the product to their shopping basket, they get a much higher score as they are a hot prospect. This process of scoring visitors is based around sets of rules.

More advanced marketers (and automated marketing systems) synchronise past purchases with repeat buying patterns and also with click behaviour and automate highly relevant messages to the visitor whether via a tailored landing page, a tailored email, sms, pop-up page or even snail mail or a phone call from customer service or a sales rep.

Augmenting customer profiles
Is done by analysing the digital body language or click behavior of a visitor. Click behaviour can include

additional activity on the website such as downloading a white paper, watching a video and also non-web behaviour such as opening (or not opening) an email. A score can also integrate purchase of other products.

Progressive profiling

PP Continually collects new information about the visitor by asking just a few new questions on each visit. For example a visitor has already volunteered their name, email and company name. On the next visit they might be asked just one question such as, 'What prompted you to visit us?' or 'Where did you first hear about us?' This data is collected via web forms which essentially add a new field(s) of data to the visitor profile. A visitor is never asked the same question twice. They will never be plagued by unnecessary repeat questions which irritate visitors significantly.

Pulling social data

This means that advanced marketing automation systems can pull or collect publicly available information from a prospect's (or customer's) social media platforms including age, gender, geography (and sometimes email address) and also deeper psychographic information such as interests and groups, hobbies, marital status, political views and friends. Comments posted/shared/liked and reviews written also present an opportunity to build a deeper more comprehensive customer profile. Logging into a website via Social Sign-On (using any of your social media passwords and names) usually gives the website owner access to a visitor or customer's social information.

Sears pulls social login
to collect a rich set of profile data from shoppers,
including interests and social graphs (friends). Using
this data in parallel with its personalization engine,
Sears offers relevant product recommendations for
shoppers based on the interests in their social profile,
as well as gift ideas for a shopper's friends based on
the birthdates and interests of those friends in her
social graph. (Olson, M., 2012) The Definitive Guide
to Collecting and Storing Social Profile Data

Adding third party data

Some marketing automations systems integrate with
third party databases such as Dun & Bradstreet B2B
databases and directories. Each new sign-up
(captured in a web form) triggers an automatic check
against a database (e.g. 'we see John Smith from
Company XYZ checking to see if he is listed in this
directory) to find, and add, a company name,
website, address, telephone number (and other
company information). See how a train company
targets ideal prospect frequent flyers using this
system.

This Is Big Data

Big Data refers to large amounts of structured and
unstructured data that require machine-based
systems and technologies to create, collect and
analyse. Data is everywhere. So too is Big Data and
more and more are starting to use it cleverly. From
supermarkets, to Lady Gaga, to Google cars to

politicians, to the FBI, to children's hospitals to detect infections before they 'occur', the list goes on.

Clustering, segmenting and profiling
Some systems will analyse a vast amount of data to see if there are any common profiles that relate to their customers (or maybe just amongst their highest spending customers). Once they have a profile they can search for other prospects with similar profiles – sometimes by using more third party databases.

Appendix 6
The Big Strategic Picture:
Kim and Mauborgne's Blue Ocean Strategy

Blue Ocean Strategy was created by Professors W.Chan Kim   Renée Mauborgne and effectively provides a 'systematic approach to making competition irrelevant and creating uncontested market space'.

Companies competing in the marketplace try to avoid the concept of 'Strategic-Hell', which occurs when it is difficult to find differentiation from competitors and price wars are unavoidable, resulting in diminishing margins,until someone gets squeezed out of the market. Blue Ocean Strategy tries to migrate from those markets and create new ones where pressure from competitors is low or nonexistent. For example Apple iPhones and Apple iPods   created new product-markets away from traditional competition.

The concept is appealing but in reality it is difficult to do. Companies need to make a constant effort to imagine how their competitive position could be improved. Blue Ocean's 'four actions' framework may help to achieve the desired position by exploring these four points: 'Eliminated', 'Reduced', 'Raised' and 'Created'. We will use the *Cirque du Soleil* ('Circus of the Sun' is a dramatic mix of circus arts and street entertainment).

ELIMINATED: Which of the factors that the industry takes for granted should be *eliminated*? *Cirque du Soleil* eliminated traditional circus themes, animals.

REDUCED: Which factors should be *reduced well below* the industry's standard? *Cirque du Soleil* reduced children focus.

RAISED: Which factors should be *raised well above* the industry's standard? *Cirque du Soleil* raised the adult focus (including corporate targeting).

CREATED: Which factors should be *created* that the industry has never offered? Created multiple productions and artistic dance.

The Big Strategic Picture: Akao's House of Quality Analysis

The house of quality is a popular name given to the Quality Function Deployment (QFD) diagram created by Yoji Akao, (1966). It is also known as 'the voice of the customer' since the purpose of the analysis is to understand why customers buy (or don't buy) a particular product or service.

The method tries to identify WHAT the customer wants or needs, and HOW it can be delivered (product/service). The WHAT is the market requirement, with the HOW being the design characteristics of the product or service.

This tool may be used as a link between the SITUATION Analysis Section and the Strategy section of SOSTAC®. Once all of the Situation Analysis is complete it is easier to see the Key Success Factors (the market requirements, the WHAT) and the Competitive Distinctive Capabilities (the HOW). The WHAT and the HOW must fit together neatly.

Consider Kodak. Customers want to take pictures (WHAT) and Kodak knows HOW (cameras). WHAT and HOW fit. Then suddenly (and disruptively), digital cameras (a substitute for film) were launched by new competitors and were rapidly adopted by customers. The new WHAT doesn't fit with the traditional KODAK's HOW. Kodak must find a new HOW (new product/service).

If Kodak's What andHow fit, the company can build on this. If they do not fit, strategic changes must be made to make them fit. Kodak needed to create a new product or service which fitted with customers WANTs, i.e. ink, printing service, printers, corporate printers, outsourcing printing services and even digital cameras.

These are strategic issues. If no correct strategic solution is found all the tactics will be wrong regardless (since the strategy will be wrong). Of course, this analysis may be carried out at different levels, e.g. by product/segment, line of products or entire product portfolio.

QFD analysis is complex, but it may be simplified creating a WHAT versus HOW matrix as illustrated in the table below.

The table helps you to see if your product or service has a sustainable competitive advantage. The first step is to prioritize the WHATs (what customers need). Since companies have limited resources and cannot satisfy all customer needs, it is important to assign importance (priority) to customer requirements.

For example, consider a generic software product such as a payment system. Here is 'WHAT' (customers need):
Security is identified as the first customer priority, followed by Fast (the service needs to be delivered quickly), followed by Responsive (it must be always available and work with no errors) and finally, Compatible (it must work on most platforms and systems).

Then align the HOWs against the WHATs, by
assessing three questions:

1. Does our HOW fit with the WHAT?
Yes (Y) or No (N).
The features of our product match (Y) or do not
match (N) with customers requirements.

2. Do competitors offer a similar capacity?
Can competitors also deliver their own HOWs
(products/service features) that match the WHAT? If
'No' then you are the only one and therefore insert
'W' in the table below (good news!). If YES, we name
the competitor (in the table).

3. Is our position sustainable (medium-long term)?
Yes means that our HOW satisfies the customer's
WHAT (now and in the medium to longer term) and
that position is likely to be maintained somehow
(technology, patents, exclusive distribution
channels). 'No' means competitors are going to take
you over soon (for example by just copying your
offering).

QFD matrix example for a software product

HOW

		Fire-wall	Availability	Stand-ards
WHAT:	Impor-tance			
Secure	1	YWY		
Fast	2		YCompetitorN	
Responsive	3			YWN
Compatible	4			NNN

Assessing 'Secure': YWY
YWY means we deliver 'WHAT' a customer requires: 'Security' by offering a product feature ('HOW'): Firewall. We are the only company offering this 'Secure' feature which is the most important feature required by our customers. We therefore score it 'Y'. Competitors don't have adequate firewalls yet (W) and we can maintain the advantage for a while (Y). YWY is the perfect score.

Assessing 'Fast': YCompetitorN
We have a solution based for example on a proprietary algorithm to authentify users (Y), but some competitors (Competitor) also have their own algorithms so it doesn't represent a true competitive advantage, i.e. there is no real competitive position to sustain (N).

Assessing 'Responsiveness': YWN
Our product fits with customers' requirement for always working (Y). We have a technology (W) that no competitor has yet (W) but since it is based on published   standards it will soon be available to

competitors so (N).

Assessing 'Compatible': NNN
'Compatible' is a customer requirement (albeit not a top priority). We don't deliver this, hence 'N'. Do competitors offer a similar capacity? No so 'N'. Is our position sustainable (medium-long term)? Obviously not as we don't offer this as a feature yet so 'N'. Note this is a feature not delivered yet and could represent an opportunity.

Note: 'N Competitor N'
Would mean that we do not satisfy this particular customer requirement ('N'). There   are competitors and obviously this is not a sustainable advantage (as we don't have one right now).

Note 'Y Competitor N'
Would mean that we satisfy this particular customer requirement but there are competitors offering it also and our advantage is not sustainable.

The products/services are composed by all the WHATs versus the HOWs. The marketing team has to evaluate if the final product is robust enough to be manufactured and marketed.

The table summarizes our competitive positioning at a detailed level and reflects visually the strong and weak points, linking Strategy with Tactics (often a difficult task) where a product or service needs to be totally defined and ready to go to the market. The analysis helps marketers to consider specific features of a product or service and identify areas for improvement (build differentiation or maintain sustainability).

HOW

		Fire-wall	Availability	Stand-ards
WHAT:	Impor-tance			
Secure	1	YWY		
Fast	2		YCompetitorN	
Responsive	3			YWN
Compatible	4			NNN

So what does the table above tell you?
The table reveals that our solution has a very small competitive advantage and we rely on one of the four most important features. The product right now, is competitive but it could fail if some changes in the environment occur, e.g. a new security standard. The table also highlights the possibility of creating a compatible platform which would work on a wide set of platforms (windows, iphones, android, symbian) which would deliver more advantage. The tool effectively helps to analyze the Competitive Advantage in detail and link it to the real features of a product.

Appendix 7
Strategy: The Marketing Process
- Do You Need To Revamp Your Marketing Department?

Campaign Manager - The campaign manager plans and executes messaging based on **buyer behavior** and customer readiness. They develop a marketing automation strategy that follows pre-determined lead scoring guidelines and list segmentation rules. It's about managing the funnel to distinguish between marketing-ready leads and sales-ready leads.

Content Strategist
Your content represents the voice of your company. Dem and generation begins with knowing your audience and buyer personas. Craft a message that not only speaks to that audience, but influences action to buy and share your ideas, products, and services.

Designer
Internet marketing is all about "visual". There was a time when catchy titles and headlines did the trick. Now designers play a big role in creating eye-catching imagery, videos, books, and site layouts that attract and guide visitors through a well planned, "by design", customer experience.

Developer   Increase visitor engagement through web apps and smart content. Developers work closely within the marketing team to increase visitor engagement through web apps and smart content. They strategically display different messaging and filter content and offers based on an individual visitor's stage in the buying cycle.

Systems Administrator   The Systems Administrator secures the integrity of customer data and is responsible for integrating software and managing workflows. The best can integrate them all, from Marketing Automation to CRM to Financials.

Analyst Standard metrics and in-depth analysis of marketing performance. They offer insights that impact decisions for future campaigns and help shape new strategies that deliver greater ROI.

Doyle Slayton (2014) 6 Talents of Modern Day Marketers, LinkedIn 13 May

Appendix 8
Control: Monitoring Your Ads Share Of Voice

Online ads – good news, Google AdWords calculates your SOV for you. Google, SOV is "a relative portion of inventory available to a single advertiser within a defined market sector over a specified time period." Google defines "inventory" as the impression inventory available against your campaign based on your keyword and campaign settings. Google AdWords Auction Insights Report allows you to compare your average position with competitors, your impression share, and the amount of times you are above them in search results. If you want to see how to go about setting up a competitor benchmarking process, see my Emarketing Excellence co-author Dave Chaffey (2013) and his Smart Insights knowledge hub.

References

Adams, P. (2014) Design futures 2: personalization and the new product canvas, Inside Intercom.io
Akhtar, O. (2014) Who is winning the Marketing Cloud wars? The Hub, 5 March
Anders, G. (2012) Jeff Bezos's Top 10 Leadership Lessons, Forbes 4 April.
Band, W. & Hagen, P. (2011) The Right Customer Experience Strategy, Destination CRM, May 2011

Barry, C., Markey, R., Almquist, E. and Brahm, C. (2011) Putting social media to work, Bain Brief, 12 Sep

Bear, J. (2013) 2 Minutes on BrightTALK: Marketing so useful people would pay for it, BrightTALK

Belicove, M (2013) Content Marketing Study Suggests Most Content Marketing Doesn't Work, Forbes 10 Sep

Benady, A. (2014) E-cigarette boss Jacob Fuller on comms and the industry's 'biggest mistake' PR Week, 25 June

Bosomworth, D. (2014) Why and how marketers must respond to the decline in organic reach, Smart Insights 19 Aug.

Bossidy, L. & Charan, R.C. (2012) Execution: The Discipline of Getting Things Done , Crown Books

Chaffey, D. & Ellis Chadwick, F. (2013) Digital Marketing: Strategy, Implementation and Practice, 5th edition © Pearson Education Limited

Chaffey, D. & Smith, PR (2013) Emarketing Excellence 4th ed., Routledge

Chaffey, D. (2013) Improve your Competitor analysis and benchmarking   Chaffey, D. (2013) Google Adwords Changes in 2013 – reviewing the opportunities and potential problems, Smart Insights 9 Aug.

Chaffey, D. (2013) Introducing RACE: a practical framework to improve your digital marketing, Smart Insights 14 Nov.

Cramer, B. (2014) How should you measure your share of voice? Ragan's PR Daily 10 Jan

Dalton (2012) How brands can leverage the power of visual social media, Media Matters, 20 Dec.

daSilva, T. (2014) Why Ignoring User Intent is Costing You Money in AdWords, Unbounce, 5 Sep

Doyle Slayton (2014) 6 Talents of Modern Day Marketers, LinkedIn 13 May

Duhigg, C. (2012) how companies learn your secrets, new york times, 16 Feb

Eloqua (2013) White Paper: Revenue Performance Management-Re-Engineering the Revenue Cycle

Erlhoff, M. & Marshall, T. (2008) Design Dictionary: Perspectives on Design Terminology, Birkhäuser Verlag

Forrester Consulting (2013) Use Behavioral Marketing To Up The Ante In The Age Of The Customer, Silverpop.

Foy, H. (2014) Have car shows run out of road? FT, 5 May

Gladstone, B. (2014) 'How To Use Twitter Advanced Search Queries for Leads' Social Media Examiner 5 June.

Goldber, C (2013) Marketing on Mobile: Why is this Platform Different?High Tech Communicator, 3 June

Gray, R. (2013) Retail Revolution, The Marketer Mar/Apr Marketing on Mobile: Why is this Platform Different?,Hgh Tech Communicator, 3 June

Hudson, J. (2014) Wired Magazine

Hudson, J. (2014) Disrupt or Die, Wired Magazine, Wired Magazine, 2 Oct

Ibrahim, M (2013) Twitter and WPP in global partnership, PR Week 14 June

Jackson, S. (2009) Cult of Analytics, Routledge

Jankowski, S. (2014) The Sectors Where the Internet of Things Really Matters, HBR Global Edition, 22 October

Kaye, K. (2013) Data Defined: What Is 'Big Data' Anyway? Ad Age, 15 Jan

Kirpatrick, D. (2013) Email Optimization: A single word change results in a 90% lift in sign-ups Emarketing Experiments Blog, 15 March

Kirpatrick, M. (2010) Google CEO Schmidt: People Aren't Ready for the Technology Revolution, ReadWrite, 4 Aug.

Laney, D. (2014) The Hidden Tax Advantage of Monetizing Your Data, Forbes 27 Mar

Lee, J (2013) Obama digital director praises social media, Yale News, 9 April

Levine, R., Locke, C., Searles, D. & Weinberger, D. (2000) The ClueTrain Manifesto, Perseus Books.

Marr, B. (2014) Facbook + WhatsApp = The Ultimate Spying Machine? LinkedIn 27 Feb

McGovern, G. (2010) The customer is a stranger, Gerry McGovern/New Thinking, 6 June

McGovern, G. (2014) Customer Convenience, Gerry McGovern/New Thinking, 28 Sep

McLellan, L. (2012), By 2017 the CMO will Spend More on IT Than the CIO
Gartner Webinars, 3 Jan.

Meinertzhagen, P. (2013) How to Calculate Share of Voice for Organic Search, The YouMoz Blog, 29 Nov

Miller, J. (2013) 5 LinkedIn Company Page Tips to Enhance Your Marketing, Social Media Examiner 23 Oct.

Muellner, M. (2013) Three 'Light Bulb Moments' to illuminate social media marketing success, Marketing Profs 31 Oct.

Murphy, J. (2013) Listening vs. Hearing: How to increase your Twitter engagement rate Bloom Worldwide, 29 July

Novo, J. WebTrends, Take 10 Series Increase Customer Retention by Analyzing Visitor Segments,

Paget, J. (2013) 'Searching For The Real Value Of Facbook Marketing, Smart Insights Oct 24

Pulizzi, J. (2013) Measuring the Impact of Your Content Marketing Strategy: The Pyramid Approach, The Content Marketing Institute, 1 June

Radcliff, C. (2014) Why you should be monitoring your brand on Twitter, Econsultancy 14 July

Roach, J. (2014) The 10-Point Social Media Policy Everyone Will Understand, Sociallogical, 2 June

Rogers, B. (2013) Seeking CMOs: Must Know Big Data and Digital Marketing, Forbes 15 Jan

Satell, G. (2014) Are We Ready For The Personal Web? Forbes 25 Jan

Satell, G. (2102) 4 Essential Questions to Ask About Your Digital Strategy, Digital Tonto, 17 Oct

Schaefer, M (2014) Content Shock: Why content marketing is not a sustainable strategy, Business Grow, 6 Jan

Seybold P. (2001) Get Inside the Lives of your customers, HBR May

Silverpop, (2013) New Study: Despite Benefits, Most Marketers Still Not Capitalizing on Behaviors, Silverpop, 10 July

Simply Measured, (2014) How To Use Facbook Data To Analyze Your Competitors

Sisario, B (2014) *Venture Will Mine Twitter for Music's Next Big Thing,* New York Times, 2 Feb.

Smith, PR (2014) 'How Integrated Content Marketing Creates Competitive Advantage, www.PRSmith.org/blog 6 Nov

Smith, PR (2014) The Rise and Fall Of Owned and Earned But Not Paid Media – World Cup Marketing Wars? www.prsmith.org/blog 27 June

Smith, PR (2011) SOSTAC® Guide To Writing The Perfect Plan, www.prsmith.org/sostac

Smith, PR and Zook, Z. (2012) Marketing Communications – integrating offline and online with social, Kogan Page

Smith, PR (2013) Gamification The Good ,The Bad and The Ugly, PR Smith Marketing Blog 22 Aug.

Smith, PR (2014) Research Driven Shock Ad Uses Magic Formula and Goes Viral PR Smith Marketing Blog, 23 Aug

Smith, PR (2013)   PR Smith Marketing Blog

Smith, PR (2013)   PR Smith Marketing Blog www.prsmith.org/blog

Solis, B. (2012) There's too much talking in social media and not enough listening and learning.

TEDTalk: Reinventing Consumer Capitalism – Screw Business as Usual

Sullivan, C (2014) 17 ways to F**k-up your AB Testing, Smart Insights 16 Sep

Takahashi, D. (2013) IBM researcher can decipher your personality from looking at 200 of your tweets, VB Science, 8 Oct

Spool, J. (2009) The $300 Million Button, User Interface Engineering, 14 Jan

Toll, E. (2014) Content Marketing Strategy – 5 Essential Tips , Champion Communications 18 Sep

Toner, L. (2014) 6 Ways Social Data Can Inform Your Marketing Strategy, Hubspot, Inbound Marketing

Urbany, J., & Davis, J. (2007). Strategic Insight in Three Circles. Retrieved January 2010, Harvard Business Review, The Magazine, November.

Urbany, J. E, & Davis, J. H. (2010). Grow by Focusing on What Matters: Strategy in 3-Circles. Vermont, USA: Business Expert Press.

Watercutter, A. (2013) How Oreo Won the Marketing Super Bowl With a Timely Blackout Ad on Twitter, Wired, 2 April
Woods, S. (2009) Digital Body Language – deciphering customer intentions in an online world, New Year Publishing.
Weintraub, M (2013) The Definitive Share Of Voice Guide: PPC, SEO, Social and Multi-Channel SOV Models, AmIClearBlog Sep 6
Young, Y. (2014) Urban Myths and Their Disastrous Effects on Marketing, Cambridge Marketing College

A Final Word

The layout of your marketing plan

Feel free to lay out your plan in whatever format you or your organisation prefers. For example, it's quite common to have an executive summary at the very start. Some organisations state big objectives (mission and vision statements) at the beginning and sometimes the major financial goals. Others prefer to see a detailed Situation Analysis dumped into the appendices at the end of the document. Regardless of the final structure, if you address each section of SOSTAC® + 3Ms, under whatever name or headings you prefer, you will have covered all the key ingredients for a great plan.

Good luck with it.
Paul Smith

PS Feedback Is Welcomed

Please do let me know what you think of this book. All feedback, suggestions for improvement and examples of how you applied SOSTAC® are most welcome. Please use the dedicated feedback section on my website www.prsmith.org/feedback . That would be very much appreciated. Many Thanks.

Keep in touch via

🔗	PRSmith.org	🔗	GreatSpotsmanship.org
f	PRSmith Marketing	f	Great Sportsmanship
🐦	@PR_Smith	🐦	@GtSportsmanship
in	PR Smith Marketing	in	Great Sportsmanship programme
▶	PRSmith1000	▶	Great Sportsmanship programme

For more on SOSTAC® workshops and webinars and registered SOSTAC® consultants and trainers visit: www.prsmith.org/sostac or if you've got examples of great marketing for the next edition, or, any feedback please got to www.PRSmith.org/feedback.
Best Wishes, Paul

V5.8 Mar 2015

14725045R00162

Printed in Great Britain
by Amazon.co.uk, Ltd.,
Marston Gate.